Bombard the Headquarters!

The Cultural Revolution in China

GREAT  EVENTS

Linda Jaivin

For Geremie

Published in Great Britain in 2025 by
Old Street Publishing Ltd
Notaries House, Exeter EX1 1AJ

www.oldstreetpublishing.co.uk

ISBN 978-1-91308-394-6
Ebook ISBN 978-1-91308-373-1

10 9 8 7 6 5 4 3 2 1

A CIP catalogue record for this title is available from
the British Library.

Printed and bound in Great Britain.

TABLE OF CONTENTS

A CULTURAL REVOLUTION TIMELINE

1949	People's Republic of China founded	End of civil war; Chiang Kai-shek flees to Taiwan
1958	Great Leap Forward	Economy collapses
1958–61	Mass famine across China	Tens of millions die; President Liu Shaoqi sidelines Mao
May 1964	'Little Red Book'	Soldiers get their copies first
Nov. 1965	Yao Wenyuan critiques play by Wu Han	Sparks culture war at the heart of the Cultural Revolution
1966		
16 May	16 May Circular	Official start of the Great Proletarian Cultural Revolution
27 May	First Red Guards	Students swear loyalty to Mao
5 August	Mao pens 'Bombard the Headquarters'	Attacks Liu Shaoqi and other Party leaders
August	Red August, beginning of revolutionary 'link-ups'	Red Guards murder 1,800 people in Beijing alone, get free travel across China to spread revolution
Late 1966	Workers join the Cultural Revolution	Zhou Enlai concerned about impact on economy
1967		
January	Shanghai Commune	Short-lived experiment in 'direct democracy'
January	Army joins Cultural Revolution	Violence ramps up
January–July	Wuhan Counter-Revolutionary Incident	Factional violence involving the army peaks in Wuhan
Sept. 1967–March 1969	Campaign against 'Inner Mongolian People's Party'	Persecution of non-existent party results in up to 100,000 deaths
1968		
April–July	'Hundred Day War'	Battles between rival Red Guard factions at Tsinghua University.

April–July (cont.)	'Hundred Day War' (cont.)	Workers help end the fighting, becoming the new revolutionary vanguard
May	'Cleansing the Class Ranks' begins	Entire families killed in rural slaughter
December	'Rustication' of youth begins	1968–1976, 16 million students are exiled to the countryside
1969		
March	Border war with USSR	Fear of nuclear war
April	Ninth Party Congress	Cultural Revolution declared over; the killing continues
Jan. 1970	One Strike, Three Antis	New campaign that will eventually claim 200,000 lives
April 1971	'Ping Pong diplomacy'	Warming of Sino-US relations
Sept. 1971	Death of Lin Biao	Mao's successor dies in mysterious plane crash
Oct. 1971	UN recognises PRC	China in, Taiwan out
Feb. 1972	Nixon visits China	Rising trade with West
May 1975	Mao criticises 'Gang of Four'	Mao's wife Jiang Qing and her radical associates chastised
8 Jan. 1976	Death of Zhou Enlai	Nationwide mourning
April 1976	Tiananmen Incident	Mass protests
9 Sept. 1976	Death of Mao	Gang of Four soon arrested
Nov. 1978	Democracy Wall movement	Brief period of free expression
Dec. 1978	Reform Era begins	Deng Xiaoping, twice purged in Cultural Revolution, is now paramount leader
1981	Trial of Gang of Four	Jiang Qing and associates imprisoned; relatively few others held to account
1981	The Party declares Cultural Revolution a mistake	Official resolution says Mao misled by 'counter-revolutionary cliques'
2012–	New Era of Xi Jinping	Discussion of Cultural Revolution increasingly censored

CAST OF CHARACTERS

* * *

Party Leadership in early 1966

Mao Zedong | Chairman of the Chinese Communist Party, founder of the People's Republic of China

Liu Shaoqi | President of the People's Republic, Mao's chief political target in the Cultural Revolution

Lin Biao | Marshal of the People's Republic, Vice Chairman and Mao's chosen successor

Zhou Enlai | Premier of the People's Republic and first foreign minister

Deng Xiaoping | Vice Premier, Liu Shaoqi ally. Will survive purges to lead the Reform Era

Tao Zhu | Head of Central Propaganda Department, fourth in Party hierarchy in May 1966, soon purged

*

Gang of Four

Jiang Qing | Mao's fourth wife (m. 1939), political operator and advocate for radical revolutionary culture

Wang Hongwen | Youngest member, worker. Reaches third place in Party hierarchy in 1973

Yao Wenyuan | Author of 1965 attack on playwright Wu Han that paves way for Cultural Revolution

Zhang Chunqiao | Member of the Cultural Revolution Group, 1967 Shanghai Commune organiser

*

Red Guards and Rebels

Kuai Dafu | Influential leader of Tsinghua Uni Red Guard faction

Nie Yuanzi | Author of big-character poster at Peking Uni that inspires 'Bombard the Headquarters'

Song Binbin | Leader of high-school Red Guards who murder their teacher in August 1966

*

Other Notables

Chen Boda | Head of Cultural Revolution Leading Group, Mao's political secretary, ally of Lin Biao

Chen Zaidao | Regional PLA commander, leader of Million Heroes in Wuhan Incident

Kang Sheng | Mao's trusted and powerful head of security, leading member of Central Case Investigation Group

Hua Guofeng | Mao's successor, ends Cultural Revolution with help of Ye Jianying and Wang Dongxing

Qi Benyu | Propagandist, member of Cultural Revolution Leading Group, aide to Jiang Qing

Wang Dongxing | Military commander, chief of Mao's personal bodyguard

Xie Fuzhi | Minister for Public Security from 1959–1972, member of radical faction

Ye Jianying | Defence Minister from 1975, supports Hua Guofeng in coup that ends Cultural Revolution

*

Prominent Victims

Lao She | Beloved novelist and dramatist, People's Artist, victim of Red Guard violence

Ulanhu | First Party Secretary of Inner Mongolian Autonomous Region

Wang Guangmei | Wife of Liu Shaoqi, Party veteran humiliated at mass struggle session on Jiang Qing's orders

Wu Han | Deputy mayor of Beijing, historian. Author of the controversial *Hai Rui Dismissed from Office* (1961)

Yu Luoke | Activist and author of 'On Class Origins', executed in 1970

Zhang Zhixin | Party member and strident critic of Mao and the Cultural Revolution, executed in 1975

*

PROLOGUE

> A revolution is not a dinner party...
> A revolution is an act of insurrection,
> an act of violence by which one class
> overthrows another.
> *Mao Zedong*

Tensions were running high on 5 August 1966. Mao Zedong and his fellow Communist Party leaders were meeting for the fifth day in a row in Beijing's Great Hall of the People. On the first day, Chairman Mao had continually interrupted the speech of the Party's number two leader, President Liu Shaoqi. On the fourth day, the two had quarrelled, Mao shouting at Liu from his seat right next to him. Mao's Great Proletarian Cultural Revolution was finally under way and the country's youth had responded to it with ferocious enthusiasm – and then, while Mao was away in the south, Liu had gone about trying to calm them down. 'You have established a bourgeois dictatorship in Beijing!' Mao accused.

At 72, the Chairman was the only delegate to have attended the founding congress of the Chinese Communist Party in 1921. Visionary, ruthless, shrewd and determined, he had weathered hardship, war and power struggles to lead that Party and then the country itself. Now, seventeen years after the birth of the People's Republic, it seemed to him that the revolution had lost its dynamism and the Party was stagnating. Keeping the revolutionary spirit alive meant incessant class struggle and the purging of footdraggers, insubordinates, opportunists and saboteurs. The display of Mao's fearsome temper would have filled many of the other 139 delegates with dread, especially when he went on to state darkly that there were 'evil elements' in that very room.[1]

A copy of the *Beijing Daily* lay on the table before him. Mao picked up a pencil and dashed off some thoughts in the

'Evil elements' in the room

1

margins. He handed it to a secretary, who tidied his words into a short text. Mao made a few more amendments. Two days later his call to arms, 'Bombard the Headquarters – My Big-Character Poster', was printed and circulated to his fellow Party leaders.

But what did Mao even mean by 'bombard the headquarters'? He was the leader of the Party – he *was* the headquarters. Or was he? As he saw it, Liu Shaoqi, along with Vice-Premier Deng Xiaoping, the Party's general secretary, had been undermining him for years. They had become a *de facto* 'opposition headquarters' within the Party. It was time for the gloves to come off.

'Bombard the Headquarters' began by praising another recent big-character poster, or *dàzìbào*. A *dàzìbào* was a political statement writ large in brush and ink and posted in a public space. Big-character posters were typically vitriolic in tone, characterised by militaristic language, the ridicule of enemies and rhetorical questions posed in a mood of high dudgeon. In the 1930s and 1940s they had promoted resistance to the Japanese invasion. There was a brief flourishing of *dàzìbào* in the mid-1950s, when Mao called on people to tell the Party what it could do better ('Let a hundred flowers bloom!'), only to dispatch many of those who tried to do so to labour camps. As a political tool the big-character poster had vanished after that – until the 45-year-old Party Secretary of Peking University's Philosophy Department, Nie Yuanzi, pasted one onto a wall of her campus on the afternoon of 25 May 1966.

Return of the big-character poster

A Party member since 1938, Nie had been fighting with university administrators for years over their reluctance to follow Mao's instructions to 'integrate theory and practice' and send students to farms and factories where peasants and workers could teach them about real life. Not highly educated herself, she was also unhappy with the way the university prioritised academic achievement over political activism, particularly when it came to promotions – such as one for which she had been overlooked. Her poster, co-signed by several others, claimed that the 'soaring revolutionary spirit' of the people was being suppressed by a 'sinister, anti-Party, anti-socialist gang'. It concluded:

2

Resolutely, thoroughly, totally and completely wipe out all ghosts and monsters and all Khrushchevian Counter-Revolutionary Revisionists and carry the socialist revolution through to the end. Defend the Party's Central Committee! Defend Mao Zedong Thought! Defend the Dictatorship of the Proletariat!

Nie's complaint about university authorities paying lip-service to Mao's teachings mirrored Mao's own frustrations with Liu Shaoqi, Deng Xiaoping and others he accused of mouthing revolutionary slogans while shackling the Party with bureaucracy. Mao felt that Khrushchev had betrayed Stalin's legacy in the Soviet Union by introducing a kind of Communism Lite. Now, he believed, Liu, Deng and others were attempting to do the same in China.

Stalin's legacy betrayed

Although a voracious reader and autodidact, Mao distrusted establishment intellectuals no less than Nie. His antipathy had deep roots in the humiliation he'd felt after first arriving in Beijing decades earlier to work in the library at Peking University, where the elite had mocked him for his thick provincial accent and earthy, peasant manners. For years, Mao had been calling for a cultural revolution against 'bureaucratism', compromise and complacency. Nie, for one, had been listening. Mao ordered the text of her *dàzìbào* to be broadcast and published nationally on 1 June, extending its influence well beyond the university gates. Nie herself would go on to play a major role in the unfurling chaos of the next ten years.

After praising Nie's big-character poster, Mao's 'Bombard the Headquarters' went on to accuse 'some leading comrades' of

> ...standing with the reactionary bourgeoisie, enforcing bourgeois dictatorship and shooting down the dynamic movement of the Great Cultural Revolution. They reverse right and wrong, confuse black and white, besiege and oppress revolutionaries, silence dissent, inflict white terror, and feel smug about it. They promote bourgeois arrogance and deflate the proletarian morale of the proletariat. Should this not wake us up?

3

'White terror' was a serious accusation. The phrase was normally used to describe the brutal persecution of Communist Party members, allies and sympathisers by the anti-communist Kuomintang (KMT) Party three decades earlier. The leader of the KMT and later president of the Republic of China, Chiang Kai-shek, had originally agreed to cooperate with the Communists before dramatically betraying them in 1927. Chiang set gangsters and thugs on unionised workers in Shanghai and pointed his own feared security forces at anyone believed to be sympathetic to the communist cause. Young students had been imprisoned, tortured or even executed. The campaign cost tens of thousands of lives, including those of most of the 60,000 members of the Party at the time. By using the phrase 'White Terror', Mao was equating resistance to his leadership with Chiang's monumental and murderous treachery.

Subsequent propaganda images depict Mao writing his declaration in big, bold characters on a poster with brush and ink – a romantic revolutionary makeover of a pencil scribble in the margins of a newspaper. Widely broadcast and circulated in print, 'Bombard the Headquarters' helped to detonate an explosion of political violence that would tear apart Chinese politics, culture and society over the following decade. The Great Proletarian Cultural Revolution promised to build a new world. It would leave the old one in tatters.

PART ONE

1949-1966: The Buildup

> Throughout history, reactionary forces threatened
> with extinction have waged a final, desperate
> struggle against the revolutionary force.
>
> *Mao Zedong*

It wasn't the first time Mao had threatened to blow up the Party over which he presided.

After the Communists established the People's Republic of China in 1949, Chiang Kai-shek fled with his government, army and followers to Taiwan. Decades of misrule, endemic corruption, foreign invasion and civil war had left China with a shattered infrastructure and dysfunctional bureaucracy. Its people were traumatised and poverty was widespread. Eighty percent of the population over the age of 15 was illiterate. There was an urgent need for hospitals, clinics and schools. Mao wanted to transform both the material conditions of the country and its ideological superstructure while eliminating all resistance, even passive resistance, to the new regime, and quickly.

Legacy of misrule

The Communist Party had developed two basic models for revolutionary action, both of which required mass participation and promoted ideological indoctrination. The first emerged from its land reform campaigns of the late 1940s, when activists had mobilised poor and landless peasants not just to seize and redistribute land held by wealthy landholders, but to hold public 'struggle sessions' where they 'spoke bitterness' (*sùkŭ*) about the past and confronted landowners over the exploitation of their labour. If they beat and sometimes even murdered their former oppressors, well, such was the nature of class struggle. Revolution, Mao had famously remarked, was not a dinner party.

5

The second model was that of the thought reform campaign, aimed at eliminating 'erroneous thinking' among the Party membership, educated people and government workers. This involved a rigorous and often brutal process of 'criticism and self-criticism', also known as 'struggle' (dòuzhēng). The first years of the 1950s saw the completion of land reform across the country and a series of thought reform campaigns to eliminate bureaucratism and other old ways of thinking and doing things.

In 1956, Mao called on the people to tell the Party how they thought it was doing: 'Let one hundred flowers bloom!' Although taken aback by the avalanche of criticism that followed, he may well have intended, as the Chinese saying has it, to 'lure the snakes out of their cave'. One year later, he launched the Anti-Rightist Campaign. Overseen by Party General Secretary Deng Xiaoping, it consigned hundreds of thousands of people to labour camps, many for answering the call to speak out the year before, and created a new category of political enemies: 'rightists'.

In 1958, Mao launched his most ambitious campaign to date, the Great Leap Forward. The idea was that radical collectivisation and mass mobilisation would propel China straight into true communism. Its economy would surpass Great Britain's and catch up with that of the United States. The whole country was organised into People's Communes. Even ploughs and the water buffalo that pulled them became communal property. The Party ordered the citizenry 'go all out and aim high' to quadruple agricultural and industrial production, encouraging measures such as the extremely dense planting of single crops and the sacrifice of family woks and metal window frames to 'backyard furnaces' to produce steel.

The Great Leap Forward

Mao excoriated the scientists and other experts who predicted catastrophic economic collapse – correctly, as it turned out. Realising that the only welcome news was good news, local officials and state media boasted of fancifully high harvests and industrial output. In the summer of 1959, the Party convened at the mountain retreat of Lushan. There, Peng Dehuai, defence minister and Mao's ally of three decades, warned of the 'winds of exaggeration' and impending food

6

shortages, saying politics shouldn't override 'economic principles'. Mao was livid. Though theoretically part of a collective leadership, he was used to calling the shots. He sacked Peng Dehuai and threatened that if the People's Liberation Army was unhappy about his decision then he, Mao, would raise a new army and overthrow his own government. He replaced Peng with the wily military man Lin Biao, of whose loyalty he felt assured.

The mass famine that ensued would claim tens of millions of lives by 1961, killing somewhere between 5 and 10 percent of the entire population of 650 million. Natural disasters contributed to the death toll, as did a rancorous split with the Soviet Union under Khrushchev that saw the Soviets halt all aid to China, but the Great Leap Forward had clearly propelled China towards disaster. Mao, personally insulated from the worst effects of famine by the Party's system of 'special provisions' for its leaders – and spared the worst news by subordinates who understood the price of truth-telling – remained unmoved. Finally, other members of the Chinese leadership took matters into their own hands.

1960–61: Capitalist Roaders, Soviet Revisionists and an Incident on a Train

In 1960, Deng Xiaoping learned that the provincial Party secretary of Anhui province, faced with potentially ten million deaths in his province alone, had assigned parcels of communal land to individual peasants. After providing the state with their assigned quota of grain, farmers could keep any excess for personal consumption or trade at local 'free markets'. They could even raise a pig or two for consumption and sale.

Deng, President Liu Shaoqi and others began promoting Anhui's 'field responsibility system' more broadly, helping to mitigate the famine. Limited financial incentives were introduced to the industrial sector as well. The economy began slowly to recover. Questioned if such a policy could still be called socialist, Deng Xiaoping allegedly replied: 'It doesn't matter if a cat is black or white. If it catches mice, it's a good cat.' This would later be cited as proof that Deng was a 'capitalist roader'.

7

Under pressure, Mao initially agreed to the field responsibility system, although he felt that it betrayed his revolutionary vision. He also believed that the quotidian tasks of government were subsuming the Party's revolutionary spirit. If revolution was not a continuous process, he argued, it would become inert and the triple evils of 'feudalism, capitalism and revisionism' would take root once more.

When Mao spoke of revisionism, he was talking about Khrushchev, who had denounced Stalin's personality cult, promoted the principle of collective leadership, freed victims of Stalinist purges from labour camps and reinvigorated the Soviet Union's consumer economy. Such policies offended Mao ideologically as much as they threatened him personally. In the 1950s, the Party had promised its citizens that 'the Soviet Union's today is our tomorrow'. Yet by the start of the 1960s, the Soviet Union of the day had come to represent Mao's worst nightmare. He would not tolerate 'Khrushchevs' and 'phony communism' within the Party he had helped to found.

Worse still, Khrushchev preached peaceful coexistence with the United States – those American imperialists whom Mao considered the 'sworn enemies of the people of the world'. In the early 1950s, Washington had signed a mutual defence treaty with Chiang Kai-shek, who continued to threaten to 'retake the mainland' from Taiwan. By the 1960s, the US army had military bases in South Korea, Japan and the Philippines. It trained and armed Tibetan guerrilla fighters and provided them with bases in Nepal. The Americans were increasingly involved in Vietnam as well. And now Russia and India were becoming friendly. 'Peaceful co-existence' sounded to Mao more like the encirclement of China by hostile forces.

Early in 1961, Mao turned his focus on his enemies within. Travelling south in his special railway carriage, he stopped in Wuhan to meet with the city's Party secretary. While he was out and about, members of his entourage and train crew took a stroll. In his memoir, *The Private Life of Chairman Mao*, Mao's personal physician Li Zhisui recalled that among their number were several of the young women whom Mao kept around for his sexual pleasure. Mao had been an early champion of women's rights, even appropriating a woman's

8

voice in a 1919 essay to complain: 'The shameless men, the villainous men, make us into their playthings...'[2] His behaviour was often at odds with his ideals, however, and his proclivities had long been a source of tension between him and his fourth wife, Jiang Qing. They were also an open secret among his entourage.

As they ambled along, a technician told one of the young women that he had heard her chiding Mao to hurry and get dressed. Shocked, she asked what else he'd heard. 'Everything,' he teased. She told Mao about the conversation. A sweep of his carriage turned up a pile of bugging equipment. He was furious. Several other leaders had once suggested installing recording devices in his train, so his every utterance could be preserved and every order faithfully transmitted. Mao had taken umbrage at the suggestion, yet it appeared they'd done it anyway. According to his doctor, 'his growing belief that there was a conspiracy against him within the highest ranks of the Party dates from here.'

Conspiracy within

1962–63: Class Struggle, Maple Bridge and the Spirit of the Rustless Screw

On the morning of 24 September 1962, at a meeting of the Central Committee, Mao declared that after more than ten years of Party rule in China, economic exploitation remained a problem. Denouncing 'the trend towards individual enterprise', he ordered the Party to focus on class struggle 'every year, every month, every day'. Class struggle, he insisted, was the motor of history; it was the key to human progress. Revolution could not rest.

Class struggle: the motor of history

The following year, the township of Fengqiao ('Maple Bridge') in Zhejiang province showed the rest of China how the people could ferret out class enemies in their midst – and solve a few practical problems at the same time. As elsewhere, local authorities were struggling with the after-effects of the famine, including poverty and dislocation as well as anger at the senseless loss of life. As resources for policing were limited, they came up with a solution both simple and cost-effective: mutual surveillance. The people would police each other. This was called 'mass dictatorship' – that is, dictatorship exercised *over* the people *by* the people themselves. It handily combined crime control with thought control, promoting ideological unity through universal participation in revolutionary activity. Mao heartily endorsed the 'Maple Bridge Experience'. So too would his successors, including Deng Xiaoping and Xi Jinping, but it was in the Cultural Revolution that mass dictatorship – in essence, mob rule – found its greatest expression.

Meanwhile, Mao's personality cult was growing. In 1961, Lin Biao instructed the *Liberation Army Daily* to publish a daily excerpt of the Chairman's writings on its front page. In May 1964, Lin Biao compiled a number of these into a book, *Quotations from Chairman Mao Zedong*, for distribution to members of the People's Liberation Army to study. Thanks to its size and distinctive red plastic cover, designed to be hard-wearing enough for army life, it became known as the Little Red Book. Mao was pleased, happily noting that it was longer than the two most famous books of quotations in the classical canon, Confucius's *Analects* and the *Dao De Jing* of the Daoist sage Laozi. Other Party leaders including Deng Xiaoping quietly criticised it for 'vulgarising' Mao's thought and turning his words into magical incantations.[3]

Model soldier and 'rustless screw' Lei Feng enjoying some quality time reading the works of Mao

Lin Biao also 'discovered' the diary of an ordinary soldier, Lei Feng, who'd died in 1962 at the age of 22 in an accident involving an army truck and a telephone pole. It was full of fervid declarations of loyalty to Mao and aspirations to be a 'rustless screw' in the revolutionary machine. Lin went on to 'find' a cache of suspiciously professional snapshots of Lei Feng cheerfully washing his comrades' clothes, polishing the hood of an army truck and performing other selfless good deeds. The good soldier Lei Feng was declared a model for the whole country to learn from. Mao, well pleased, called on the whole country to 'learn from the People's Liberation Army'.

In 1963–64, Mao launched a Socialist Education Campaign to root out 'bourgeois hangers-on', 'speculators', 'swindlers' and other class enemies and to eliminate economic inequality – 'this ulcer that socialism inherited from capitalism'. Four Clean-Ups were needed: of politics, ideology, organisation (bureaucracy) and the economy. The campaign resulted in a widening rift between Mao and Liu Shaoqi, who argued that the campaign should not focus on class. Liu had been an early architect of the Mao personality cult in the 1940s. But his advocacy of orderly process and persuasion over class struggle was increasingly at odds with Mao's goals of 'mass dictatorship' and continuous revolution.

Four Clean-Ups

The Socialist Education Campaign and Four Clean-Ups would result in the punishment of over five million Party members. It was during this time that the phrase *wénhùa gémìng*, 'cultural revolution' – a phrase introduced by iconoclastic thinkers in the early twentieth century – gained new currency.

1964: Staging the Revolution for a New Generation

On National Day, 1 October 1964, the fifteenth anniversary of the founding of the PRC, some 3,000 actors, dancers, singers and musicians mounted the stage at the Great Hall of the People in Beijing to perform the new revolutionary epic *The East is Red*. Inspired by monumental North Korean stage extravaganzas, it told the story of Chinese history from the Opium Wars of the nineteenth century through to the Communist victory of 1949, when the peasants and workers finally overthrew their oppressors to become masters of their own destiny. The spectacle credited the revolutionary transformation to Mao alone, whose image, at a climactic moment, rises to join those of Marx and Lenin above the stage. No other leaders were mentioned. The title song likened Mao to the sun: 'The East is red, the Sun is rising, China has produced a Mao Zedong'.

Chinese Premier Zhou Enlai liked the song and dance epic so much he saw it eleven times. A film version was soon in the works. Not everyone in the audience was impressed, however. Mao's wife Jiang Qing for one didn't consider *The East is Red* sufficiently Red enough.

At fifty, Jiang was tired of being sidelined from power. It was a compromise she'd agreed to when Mao upset his colleagues by divorcing his third wife, a veteran revolutionary, to marry her in 1939. A complex character, tough and ambitious, Jiang had grown up amid grinding poverty and violence. Her father once broke one of her teeth with a spade. Jiang had joined the Party in 1933, living a double life as a stage and film actor in Shanghai and a member of the Communist underground.

Field of dreams: stock characters from the new 'revolutionary model operas', as approved by Jiang Qing, with the Communist stronghold of Yan'an in the background

In the 1950s, Jiang had headed the film section of the Party's Propaganda Department, nurturing ideas about how to revolutionise Chinese culture. Building on earlier reforms, she worked with composers and writers to create stirring stories of class struggle and revolutionary triumph. The emperors, generals, 'scholars and beauties' of traditional opera yielded the stage to workers, peasants and soldiers, 'the real creators of history and the true masters of our country'. Elements borrowed from Western classical music and ballet heightened the drama. These new works were intended to remind Chinese youth of how much previous generations had sacrificed for socialism and inspire fervour.

Jiang Qing called these productions *yàngbǎnxì*, usually translated as 'revolutionary model operas' in English, although not all were operas. The precision of the stage directions for *yàngbǎnxì* did not allow for personal interpretation. Not even the size and colour of the patches on a peasant hero's costume should vary from one performance to the next. Under the Party's direction, other new cultural artefacts such as *Rent Collection Courtyard*, an installation of 114 life-size figures portraying peasants 'struggling' an exploitative landowner, were similarly designed as models (*yàngbǎn*) for precise reproduction.

Nyet means nyet

Soviet Premier Alexei Kosygin arrived in Beijing in February 1965 to talk about America's growing presence in Vietnam and to invite Mao and others to attend a summit in Moscow the following month. He suggested that the two countries put a halt to their 'open dispute'. Mao wasn't interested, saying, 'I support an open dispute. The open dispute will last for another ten thousand years.' Kosygin suggested that it didn't need to last so long. Mao countered: 'nine thousand' then.

A Soviet overture rebuffed

Mao's intervention threw into disarray arrangements by Kosygin and Zhou Enlai to promote bilateral trade and scholarly exchange and for the Soviets to complete aid projects in China abandoned after the Sino-Soviet split five years earlier. Mao did not want to be seen to be compromising with 'Soviet revisionists', especially when he was on the verge of launching the cultural revolution he'd been ruminating on for several years now.

Everyone's a Critic

Nearly four centuries after his death, a principled official of the Ming dynasty named Hai Rui became the unlikely protagonist of the unfolding political drama. Hai Rui had famously remonstrated with a sixteenth century emperor for neglecting

13

his people's welfare. The emperor had wanted to execute Hai Rui, but died first.

Mao saw himself as Hai Rui, an official fighting for the masses against an entrenched bureaucracy. On the eve of the Great Leap in 1958, Mao had suggested to Wu Han, the deputy mayor of Beijing and a Ming historian, that he explore this theme in writing. Among the works Wu Han produced was a play called *Hai Rui Dismissed from Office*, finishing it in 1961, towards the end of the Great Famine.

Hai Rui Dismissed from Office

Mao came to suspect that Wu Han intended the righteous Hai Rui to represent the sacked army chief Peng Dehuai while the cruel emperor stood for him. Other writers at the time were employing similar literary allusions and historical allegories as veiled criticisms of Mao. Many of their essays were published in *Front Line*, the journal of the Beijing Municipal Party Committee overseen by Wu Han's boss, mayor Peng Zhen. Beijing was beginning to feel like enemy territory to Mao.

In 1965, Wu Han published the biography of another major historical figure, Zhu Yuanzhang, the peasant rebel who founded the Ming dynasty in 1368. Wu Han wrote how the rebel-turned-emperor was prone to violent purges and ultimately betrayed his poor and oppressed supporters.

By September 1965, Mao had had enough. He demanded that the Party condemn Wu Han and renew its fight against 'reactionary bourgeois ideology'. On 10 November, the Shanghai newspaper *Wenhui Daily* published a strident critique of Wu Han's play. The author was Yao Wenyuan, a young radical from Shanghai and an associate of Mao's wife. Yao would become part of the tight-knit, ultra-radical group around Jiang Qing that would eventually be labelled the Gang of Four. Yao described *Hai Rui Dismissed from Office* as 'a deliberate, planned and organised' attack on the Party and socialism.

Mao wanted Yao's article published in Beijing. Mayor Peng Zhen, who ranked fifth in the ruling Politburo and since early 1965 had headed the Group of Five charged with preparing for cultural revolution, tried to block the reprint of Yao's article in the Beijing press. Overriding him, defence chief Lin Biao saw that it appeared in both the *People's Liberation Army Daily* and the *Beijing Daily*. The tide was turning.

While demonstrating his loyalty to Mao, Lin Biao also settled a few scores. Luo Ruiqing was PLA chief of staff, a general of the highest rank, a veteran of the Long March and Korean War and a vice-premier. But he'd reportedly been implicated in the bugging of Mao's train and Lin Biao disliked him for reasons of his own. When in December 1965 Mao described Luo as an 'ambitious schemer', Lin Biao had the excuse he needed to remove the 59-year-old from his military post.

With Lin's help, Mao was consolidating his power over the army as well as the Party. About to embark on the biggest campaign of his life, he needed loyalists in all key positions.

1966: Countdown to Chaos

In March, Luo Ruiqing was accused of being part of Peng Zhen's 'anti-Party clique'. He jumped out of a window, one of the first of many suicides and near-suicides at all levels of society and government over the following decade. He survived but broke both legs, one of which eventually had to be amputated.

That same month, Mao sabotaged the Party's relations with one of its most steadfast international allies, the Japanese Communist Party. A Japanese delegation, welcomed by Premier Zhou in front of 16,000 people, spent weeks working with Liu Shaoqi and Deng Xiaoping on a joint communique expressing solidarity with Vietnam over the United States. At the eleventh hour, Mao torpedoed the agreement because the Japanese refused to call out Soviet revisionism. The Japanese communists severed relations with the Chinese party.

Split with Japanese communists

On 18 April, the army newspaper, *Liberation Daily*, warned that tolerating bourgeois culture would lead to a capitalist restoration. The Party's Central Committee, under Mao's direction, disbanded Peng Zhen's Group of Five as well as the Beijing Municipal Party Committee itself.

Many historians mark 16 May 1966 as the start of the Cultural Revolution. That day, the Party produced a document drafted by Jiang Qing and revised by Mao, initially for internal circulation to Party, state, army and cultural organisations. It was only made fully public a year later, although subsequent events, including Mao's 'Bombard the Headquarters', released less than three months later, would lay bare the power struggle at its core.

According to the 16 May Circular, 'counter-revolutionary revisionists' had infiltrated the Party, government, army and cultural circles. These hidden 'Khrushchevs' were 'sleeping beside us'. They 'waved the Red Flag to oppose the Red Flag', pretending to support the Party while scheming to restore bourgeois capitalism. The dictatorship of the proletariat had to prevail. There was no room for 'kindness or magnanimity' when dealing with class enemies. It was time to fight these monsters ('cow spirits and snake demons') including in the media, arts and universities.

16 May Circular

The contest was existential: 'Either the East Wind prevails over the West Wind or the West Wind prevails over the East Wind'. A high tide of revolution was washing across the globe. With its new Great Proletarian Cultural Revolution, the Communist Party of China under Mao would lead the international proletariat to revolution.

This was not up for debate. Lin Biao declared ominously that 'one word from Mao is equal to ten thousand words from others' and that 'the whole Party will put to death anyone who opposes Mao and the whole country will curse them'. A few days later, Premier Zhou Enlai added that if anyone was disloyal to Mao, all their previous contributions to the Party and revolution would count for nothing.

* * *

The writer Deng Tuo was Beijing Party secretary for culture, a former editor-in-chief of the *People's Daily* and a committed Maoist. Now attacked as a 'backstage manipulator' and 'class enemy' for his association with Peng Zhen among other things, he killed himself with an overdose of sleeping pills the day after the Circular came out. The act of suicide was seen as an implicit rebuke of the revolutionary order, an anti-Party, even counter-revolutionary act.

In 1919, a 25-year-old Mao had written an essay in which he blamed the tragedy of a young woman who'd slit her own throat rather than endure an arranged marriage on the social and political injustice of her time. But now the Communist Party was in charge – how could there be any social and political injustice? Thirty years on, Mao argued that no one should save a person trying to commit suicide: 'China is such a populous nation, it is not as if we cannot do without a few people.'[4] During the Cultural Revolution, the bodies of suicides would be disrespected, their families punished and mourning forbidden.

A clue to Mao's callousness lies in the historical figures for whom he expressed admiration. They included some of China's most reviled and brutal tyrants, whose cruelty he considered justified by their achievements in terms of conquest, unification, social reform or public works. To his mind, the People (*rénmín*, the revolutionary masses in the abstract) always took precedence over the individual person (*gèrén*).

* * *

That same month, the Party established a Central Cultural Revolution Leading Group. It also set up a Central Case Investigation Group to purge 'counter-revolutionary revisionists' from the top leadership. Every workplace and local government was required to set up similar groups. Only the PLA was exempt.

The Cultural Revolution Leading Group was headed by Chen Boda, Mao's political secretary and a leading Party theoretician. Other members included Mao's wife Jiang Qing, the Shanghai literary critic Yao Wenyuan and another of Jiang's Shanghai associates, the theorist Zhang Chunqiao. Kang Sheng, Mao's Machiavellian head of intelligence and security, was also a member. Kang, who'd first endeared himself to Mao by supporting his marriage to Jiang Qing when others opposed it, also ran the Central Case Investigation Group.

Cultural Revolution Leading Group

The group met at Diaoyutai, a former Qing dynasty imperial waystation, in a building revamped in the 1950s to accommodate Khrushchev when Sino-Soviet relations were still cordial. It took over the Party mouthpiece, the *People's Daily*. On 1 June, the paper editorialised that with 'the tremendous and impetuous force of a raging storm', the revolutionary masses were at last smashing 'the shackles imposed on their minds by the exploiting classes' and turning to dust the prestige of bourgeois 'specialists', 'scholars', 'authorities' and 'venerable masters'.

17

PART TWO

1966: Towards Civil War

> With struggle comes sacrifice, and it is
> common that people die.
> *Mao Zedong*

On 27 May 1966, seven students of the elite Tsinghua University Attached Middle School met by the tumbled columns and marble ruins of the Yuanmingyuan, the Qing palace sacked and burned by French and British troops in 1860 during the Opium Wars. Those wars had threatened the survival of the Qing dynasty. Now, these students believed, counter-revolutionary and 'revisionist' forces were menacing the survival of New China. Mao, China's saviour and their idol, had signalled that he was under attack. Primed for heroic action by romantic revolutionary propaganda such as *The East is Red*, full of the idealism, energy and verve of youth, they vowed to protect Mao and the revolution with their lives. They called themselves 'Red Guards' after the Russian paramilitary forces of the 1917 October Revolution. They would not just safeguard their hero but help to realise his dream of inspiring global revolution.

One of the seven, Luo Xiaohai, would describe their mission in soaring, if violent, terms:

> Revolutionaries are Monkey Kings, their golden rods are powerful, their supernatural powers far-reaching and their magic omnipotent, for they possess Mao Zedong's great invincible Thought. We wield our golden rods, display our supernatural powers and use our magic to turn the old world upside down, smash it to pieces, pulverise it, create chaos and make a tremendous mess, the bigger the better! Today we must rebel against Tsinghua Middle

School, rebel in the extreme, rebel to the end. We must create great revolutionary uproar in heaven and kill our way to a new proletarian world![5]

In a poem written several years earlier, Mao had likened himself to Sun Wukong, the wrathful and unpredictable Monkey King of the Ming dynasty novel *Journey to the West*. Most young people would have seen the 1960 film 'The Monkey King Battles the White-Boned Demon' and the 1964 animated feature 'Creating Chaos in the Heavenly Palace'. Sun Wukong, righteous in purpose and inventive in battle, was the original, literal 'chaos monkey'.

When Mao saw Luo's essay, he praised it. A whole generation of Monkey Kings was exactly what was required for continuous revolution. Luo Xiaohai himself eventually became distressed by the ensuing violence, disillusioned with the Cultural Revolution and, ultimately, with socialism itself. At the time, however, his was one of the voices that powerfully urged China's youth onto the path of mayhem and bloodshed.

A generation of Monkey Kings

The Red Guard movement, also inspired by Nie Yuanzi's example, began by denouncing teachers and school administrators as 'reactionary academics' in *dàzìbào* hung from balconies and pasted onto the walls of their schools. Such verbal attacks on teachers were shocking in the context of a culture that for millennia had venerated learning. Students visited each other's schools to copy the posters and learn how to form their own Red Guard groups. Copying *dàzìbào* helped to spread not just ideas, but the formulas for expressing them and the names of targeted individuals.

State media under the control of the Cultural Revolution Group praised their actions: 'Like sharp swords and daggers, these big-character posters pierce the enemy's vulnerable points, wound the enemy where it hurts, strengthen the resolve of revolutionaries and destroy the enemy's prestige.' The overheated rhetoric of the time recalled the millennial fervour of the Taiping Rebellion of the mid-nineteenth century, also led by a charismatic leader. That conflict had left more than 20 million dead. Mao considered it an exemplary peasant uprising.

20

Almost from the start, there were rifts in the movement. The first Red Guards came from the families of the revolutionary elite. They insisted that anyone who wanted to join them had to come from the Five Red Categories of revolutionary families – poor and 'lower middle' peasants, workers, revolutionary soldiers, revolutionary cadres and revolutionary martyrs. Anyone with a family background from the Five Black Categories – landlords, rich peasants, counter-revolutionaries, bad elements and 'rightists' (however ambiguous some of these categories were) – was automatically a class enemy and could not be a Red Guard.

The 'bloodlines theory' was summed up by the popular expression, 'The son of a revolutionary father is a hero, the son of a reactionary father a bastard.' It didn't matter that all young people were born and raised under communism, or that many of those who weren't 'born red' wanted to rebel too. It didn't even matter that official policy insisted a person's political status was distinct from their family or class origin. Bloodlines mattered.

Bloodlines theory

Other issues divided the radical young too. Some advocated non-violent action, others maximal violence. Beatings of teachers and other targets had already begun. Personal grudges and loyalties, interpretations of the ideological scripture and arguments over who was most loyal to Mao also caused ructions. Amidst the mounting chaos, classes were cancelled, as were the examinations for university admissions.

Mao went on a trip to the south. While he was away, Liu Shaoqi and Deng Xiaoping sent 'work teams' onto campuses in Beijing and other cities to try to calm things down and establish some guardrails around the process of 'struggle'. Liu Shaoqi's glamorous and well-educated wife, Wang Guangmei, headed the work team at Tsinghua University, home to some of the most fanatical Red Guards.

Mao saw these work teams as confirmation of Liu and Deng's treachery. It was time to reassert his power and show the country that at 72 he was still vigorous enough to lead a major campaign. On 16 July, in a supreme act of political theatre, Mao plunged into the Yangtze River, showing off his physical fitness while urging China's youth to 'swim against the tide' and become true successors to revolution. State media outdid itself in praise, claiming he'd swum fifteen kilometres at speeds that, even considering the current, would have surpassed those of China's 2012 Olympic champion Sun Yang.[6] According to his physician, who swam with him, he mostly just floated belly up with the current.

Chinese youth 'swim against the tide'. A year after Mao's heroic dip, more than 5,000 enthusiasts took to the Yangtze amid floating portraits of the Great Helmsman and slogans wishing him a '10,000-year' life.

Back in Beijing, Mao declared that history proved that anyone who suppressed a student movement would come to a bad end. He authorised the Central Cultural Revolution Group to recall Liu and Deng's work teams and replace them with more radical ones.

On 28 July, Jiang Qing, who would quickly rise to become one of the dominant personalities of the era alongside Mao, Zhou Enlai and Lin Biao, met with a delegation of Red Guards. Now in charge of cultural production within the People's Liberation Army, Mao's wife wore an army uniform. She would soon go from having no place in the Party's official hierarchy to No. 25, and would continue to climb as the Cultural Revolution progressed, even as Mao's marital attentions waned. She told the Red Guards that violence against 'bad people' was fine by her husband: 'If good people beat bad people, it serves them right; if bad people beat good people, the good people achieve

22

glory. If good people beat good people, it is a misunderstanding. Without beatings, you do not get acquainted...'[7]

Less than a week later, Mao confronted Liu Shaoqi at the Central Committee meeting in Beijing, accusing the work teams of 'suppressing and blocking the masses'. Soon after that, he composed 'Bombard the Headquarters!'

As author of the modern textbook on guerrilla warfare, Mao was quick to recognise and exploit opportunities. He did not create the Red Guards but immediately understood their strategic value as a tool for advancing the Cultural Revolution and purging his enemies. Once he'd broadcast his support for their movement – and sanctioned its violence – it exploded across the country. Students in every primary and middle school, university and training college across the country scrambled to form Red Guard groups. They gave themselves names like Red Flag Regiment and Rebel Corps, making their own rules about who could belong. Within three months, there would be some 15 to 20 million Red Guards in all. Some were already in university; others were as young as ten. Their rallying cry came from a recent statement by Mao: 'The myriad threads that make up the principles of Marxism come down to one thing: *To rebel is justified.*'

Early the following year, Premier Zhou Enlai added a caveat: 'Power should be seized from below, but only according to Mao's directions from above.'[8]

Red August
Bian Zhongyun was deputy principal at the Experimental High School attached to Beijing Normal University. She had been a Party member since 1941, a fervent Maoist and former editor of the *People's Daily*. But once, when explaining evacuation procedures in case of an earthquake, a student had asked if they should take Mao's portrait with them and she had said no. By 5 August, the day Mao wrote 'Bombard the Headquarters!', Red Guards had already ransacked her home, burned her books, smashed her things and plastered the walls of her home with posters threatening to 'whip her dog hide, rip out her dog heart and lop off her dog head'.[9] On that day, a group of female students brutally tortured Bian, beating her

to death with improvised weapons including nail-studded planks of wood.

It was not the first murder by Red Guards. On 3 August, Nanjing Normal University students had viciously beaten and 'struggled' Li Jingyi, the dean of studies and deputy Party secretary, and her husband Wu Tianshi, director of the provincial education department. They dragged the pair's unconscious bodies down the street until Li died, her body 'reduced to mangled flesh'. The Red Guards took Wu back to campus and continued to torture him until his arms were broken, his legs were paralysed and his brain had swelled. He died in a coma on 5 August.[10]

On 6 August, Jiang Qing addressed Red Guards at the capital's Tianqiao Theatre. She passed on Chairman Mao's regards to the students. 'We have a big enemy to deal with,' she told them, 'and we must sweep away all monsters and demons. I'm sure you'll do a good job.' What if their parents were among the capitalist roaders or the demons, one asked. Simple, she told them: 'Rebel.'[11]

'Sweep away all monsters and demons'

Among the young people who denounced their parents was the son of the Beijing film director Chen Huaikai. As Red Guards tormented his father, a fourteen-year-old Kaige joined in the chants of 'Down with Chen Huaikai!' and, mounting the stage, gave his father a shove. The shame and confusion of that betrayal would be a theme to which an older Chen Kaige would return time and again in his own work as director. In his Palme d'Or-winning 1993 film *Farewell My Concubine*, one of the main characters says: 'You just think that those vile types have brought disaster raining down on us? That's not it, no. No way! We've done it to ourselves, bit by bit, step by step.'

On 8 August, the Central Committee published *The Sixteen Points: Guidelines for the Great Proletarian Cultural Revolution*. While advocating for the use of persuasion over force, it featured many of the slogans that would be repeated endlessly over the next decade: 'Struggle against and crush people in power taking the Capitalist Road','Hold high the great red banner of Mao Zedong Thought', 'Put politics in command!' and 'Trust the masses!'

Mao decided it was time to meet and energise the masses in

person. There was no better place than Tiananmen Square, the recently expanded plaza cum parade ground just south of the old Imperial City. At about 40 hectares including surrounding structures, it was roughly the size of 100 American football fields and could fit a million people at a tight squeeze.

Tiananmen Square on 15 Sept. 1966, the third of eight mass rallies for Red Guards that year

Be Militant!

In the small hours of 18 August, a million Red Guards, brimming with revolutionary fervour, many dressed in khaki like the soldiers they considered themselves to be, packed into Tiananmen Square. As the sun came up and the oven-like heat of the Beijing summer began to build, they waved their 'Little Red Books' and shouted themselves hoarse, a continuous roar of 'Long live Chairman Mao!' By the time Mao mounted the podium at 5 a.m. wearing a military uniform, surrounded by hundreds of select Red Guards and with Lin Biao at his side, the young people in the square had entered a state akin to mass hysteria.

In 1957, Mao had said of China's youth that they were 'full of vigour and vitality, in the bloom of life, like the sun at eight or nine in the morning'. He told them: 'Our hope is placed on you. The world belongs to you. China's future belongs to you.' Still, he'd worried that those who had been born into socialism would take it for granted. As he confessed to the sympathetic American journalist Edgar Snow, he feared that China's educated youth could 'negate the revolution'. After all, they 'had never fought a war'.

Now, they had their war. In one of the Cultural Revolution's most iconic moments, the 17-year-old Red Guard Song Binbin, daughter of a Party elder, pinned an armband on Mao. She was affiliated with the group that had beaten and

25

tortured Bian Zhongyun to death. On hearing her name (*binbīn* means 'gentle and refined'), Mao suggested she change it to '*yàowǔ*' ('be militant').

The following day, state media published an article under the byline Song Yaowu proclaiming that 'violence is truth'. (Song Binbin later claimed her name and image had been hijacked.) The struggle sessions became ever more violent. Red Guards whipped their targets with heavy-buckled belts. They forced them into stress positions such as the 'airplane' (bent at the waist at 90 degrees with arms straight behind), hung heavy placards listing their crimes around their necks and propped hefty dunce caps on their heads. Some poured boiling water over their victims, electrocuted them, forced them to eat nails or excrement or made them crawl on broken glass or live embers.

'Long live the Red Terror!' was a popular Red Guard slogan. The Minister of Public Security Xie Fuzhi – a comrade of Song Binbin's father – warned police not to hinder the Red Guards: 'I do not approve of the masses killing people, but the masses' bitter hatred toward bad people cannot be discouraged, and it is unavoidable.'[12] By the end of 'Bloody August', Red Guards had murdered nearly 1,800 people in Beijing alone. The Beijing crematorium couldn't keep up with the number of corpses. With the help of security forces, Red Guards also chased some 77,000 'class enemies' out of their homes in the capital. It is estimated that at least 400,000 people were expelled from cities nationwide – frogmarched barefoot in some cases, spat on, necks bent under their heavy placards.

Meeting in mid-August, the Central Committee declared

Bloodbath in Beijing

that 'an invigorating revolutionary atmosphere prevails in the whole country'. Mao had 'raised' Marxism-Leninism to a whole new level and neither the Khrushchevian 'revisionists' in Moscow nor the US imperialists, with their war of aggression in Vietnam, could hold back the tide of 'world revolution'. The movement soon spilled from schools into workplaces, from the centre to the periphery, from the cities to the countryside. Once the 'cow demons and snake spirits' within a work unit were identified, they were herded into 'cowsheds', makeshift prisons within the workplace or its dorms, from which they could be brought out for 'struggle' or taken for 'labour reform'. These were typically crowded and decorated with Mao quotations and slogans, including the ominous 'confess and be treated with leniency; resist and be treated with severity.'

Cowsheds for the cow demons

There were eight Red Guard rallies in Tiananmen between 18 August and 26 November, attended by some 11 million Red Guards in total. At Mao's behest, Premier Zhou Enlai welcomed young people from throughout China to come to the capital to learn to make revolution. Among the students attending the second rally on 31 August was a ten-year-old girl called Liu Xiaoqing, who had made it all the way to Beijing from her home in southwestern Sichuan province. She later recalled the long wait on the square, then how the 'earth shook' as loudspeakers suddenly roared into life. Drums beat and the crowd surged forward as Mao himself, 'tall as the heavens' approached in an open limousine. She wept tears of joy: 'I was drunk on happiness... I forgot everything, my studies, my future. Life seemed so unimportant, irrelevant. Nothing could compare with this instant, because I had seen him!'[13] Another Red Guard declared the day of the rally he attended to be his true birthday.

Smash the Four Olds

In 1949, Mao had promised that the Communists would not just be 'good at destroying the old world, we will prove to be good at building a new one'. At that first Red Guard rally on 18 August, Defence Minister Lin Biao instructed the Red Guards to 'smash the Four Olds' (old ideas, culture, customs and habits) to make way for the creation of a new revolutionary

27

culture. According to Lin Biao, 'Armed struggle can only touch the flesh; only cultural struggle can touch the soul.'

Red Guards rampaged through temples, churches and mosques, smashing Buddhas and other religious icons and torturing the faithful. They ransacked museums and threw books from both public and private libraries into bonfires. They vandalised imperial tombs, even digging up the grave of Snow Brow, a Ming emperor's pet cat. Keeping goldfish, caged birds or ornamental flowers counted as 'old customs' that were signs of bourgeois self-indulgence. They forbade doctors from using foreign words in their scripts.

Loudhailers blared quotations, revolutionary songs and exhortations from morning to night. Every street was plastered with big-character posters and covered in Mao's quotations. The streets had new names, too. In Beijing, Chang'an (Eternal Peace) Boulevard became East is Red Boulevard; the city's Union Hospital, founded by the Rockefeller Foundation in 1915, became Anti-Imperialist Hospital; while the street in front of the Soviet embassy was renamed 'Anti-Revisionism Road'. Cities had so many 'Oppose Imperialism' and 'Liberation' streets that directions became futile. In their efforts to 'make the whole world red', Red Guards demanded the rewiring of traffic lights so that red signalled go; it took Zhou Enlai hours to persuade them it would be too dangerous.

The radicals disapproved of traditional expressions of femininity. Red Guards busted up hair salons and dressmakers' shops and attacked women wearing makeup, perfume and tight clothes. Female Red Guards typically wore short bobs or plaits and military uniforms belted at the waist. The model of womanhood was the 'iron girl': strong, sexless, passionate only for revolution, working with gusto whether on the farm, the assembly line, the front line or (as in a famous propaganda poster) a high-tension power line. One exception to the clench-fisted fierceness of female representation in propaganda was that of the empathetic young 'barefoot doctor', a paramedic bringing basic medical care to villages and remote areas.

On 24 August, revolutionary rebels put an emperor himself on trial. Wang Shuhua, a tour guide at the Ming Tombs, led Red Guards to unearth the skeletons of the Wanli emperor and his two empresses. The Red Guards, local peasants and others then screamed accusations at these 'ancestors of the landlord class' before attacking and burning their remains. Wang was promoted to the head of the Ming Tombs' Revolutionary Committee that would now run the site.[14]

For five centuries and two dynasties, the Forbidden City in the heart of Beijing had served as the imperial palace. Its Hall of Central Harmony had already been converted into a People's Lounge where museum workers studied Mao's thoughts and directives. The Red Guards wanted to destroy the palace completely. But when one group tried to ram its heavy red gates with a truck, Zhou Enlai commanded them to desist. He closed the palace and ordered in soldiers to protect it. Such was the ongoing threat that troops remained garrisoned inside the Forbidden City for five years. Red Guards had to content themselves with plastering its walls with *dàzìbào* calling for the 'Palace of Blood and Tears' to be burnt to the ground.

'Palace of Blood and Tears'

Rebel workers within the complex damaged religious statuary and installed a copy of the revolutionary model sculpture *Rent Collection Courtyard* in the imperial Hall for Worshipping Ancestors. They forced the museum's deputy director, the scholarly Shan Shiyuan, to stand next to the statue of the evil landowner in the installation, whom he resembled physically. Red Guards slapped Shan around so viciously that they left him partially blind.

Jiang Qing produced her own list of enemies, including former lovers from her time in the Shanghai film world, women who had caught Mao's ever-roaming eye and even an actress who'd won a role that Jiang had coveted. Others on the list included some women Party veterans she believed had conspired to keep her away from political power. Public security forces helpfully pointed Red Guards to their homes.

Jiang's hit list

* * *

Petite, witty and cosmopolitan, Nien Cheng was the wife of a former KMT diplomat who worked for the British Shell Corporation in Shanghai. The Party welcomed the couple to stay in China after the revolution and, with an eye on ensuring full employment, encouraged them to retain their servants. Nien Cheng, who held a postgrad degree from the London School of Economics, joined the company with the Party's blessing after her husband's death in 1957. Her background and situation made her an inevitable target.

The Red Guards rampaged through her house, cutting up her evening dresses, demolishing furniture, slashing mattresses, pouring medicines down the sink and smashing classical music records. When they went to stomp on rare porcelain from the reign of the Kangxi emperor (1661–1722), she tried to stop them and got a boot in the chest for her efforts. The priceless artefacts, they told her, were but 'useless toys of the feudal Emperors and the modern capitalist class' with no significance to 'us, the proletariat class'. In *Life and Death in Shanghai*, she recalled thinking that perhaps, if she were young and working class, she'd do the same. She also remembered some of the Red Guards performing small acts of kindness – quietly saving some of her nicer cardigans and undergarments – though they challenged her for eating a breakfast of toast, a 'foreign food'. She pointed out that tomatoes and watermelon were foreign foods too, and anyway, Karl Marx was a foreigner.

Nien Cheng was eventually charged with being a British spy, beaten, abused, cuffed and subjected to months of interrogations. She would spend nearly seven years in prison, during which time her daughter committed suicide.

* * *

In all, the Red Guards ransacked some 10 million homes nationwide. In many cases, they were looking for evidence – guns or money – that would prove their victims were secret agents working for Chiang Kai-shek in Taiwan, or part of a conspiracy led by President Liu Shaoqi and others to carry out a coup d'état against Mao. They rifled through closets and dug up courtyards. Many people pre-emptively burnt their own books, diaries, personal photographs and letters and even antique scrolls and valuable manuscripts, terrified of the consequences of being caught with them.

No part of the country, from remote villages to far-flung regions such as Tibet and Xinjiang, was immune from the 'Red Terror'. In Tibet, both ethnic Tibetan and Chinese Red Guards carrying red-tasselled spears attacked monks and traditional

Hunting for fifth columnists

medicine practitioners, burned temples and smashed religious icons. They used precious scripture for wrapping paper and made bonfires of sacred texts. They ripped the golden eaves and decorations off temple roofs with hoes before blowing up the temples with explosives. Red Guard factions fought a pitched

Smashing the Four Olds: Buddhist texts destroyed by Red Guards at Jokhang Temple, Lhasa, Tibet.

battle inside the Jokhang Temple, one of Tibetan Buddhism's most sacred sites, which they left in a state of ruination. The historical rebellions of the Tibetans against Chinese rule, the flight of the Dalai Lama to India in 1959 and the portrayal in Chinese propaganda of traditional Tibetan culture as 'feudal' fuelled an orgy of destruction that was worse in Tibet than almost anywhere else even if, by 1966, most of the region's monasteries had already been destroyed.

Similar scenes of political, cultural and religious devastation occurred in Xinjiang and Inner Mongolia as well. In Muslim-majority Xinjiang, the Red Guards forced Muslims to eat pork and turned mosques into piggeries.

In early 1967, the Party would make a more concerted effort to preserve precious books, artworks and furniture from the rampage, ordering Red Guards to hand them over to cultural institutions such as libraries and museums. The logic given was that if everything was destroyed, there would be no more 'old culture' to struggle against. By September 1967, Shanghai cultural institutions alone would recover some 280,000 antiques and 360,000 books and retrieve 4,000 kilos of bronze items from scrap metal plants. These were put into safe storage – or in the lingo of the time, 'returned to the People'.[15] Mao's security chief Kang Sheng, a connoisseur and aesthete, skimmed some of the most exquisite items off the top of the haul for his own delectation.

Preserving culture for future struggle

The destruction of 'old culture' extended to those who created or performed it. The Red Guards broke the fingers of a famous classical pianist. They lashed the playwright Wu Han to a tree, whipping him with their belts. The former Beijing deputy mayor endured no less than a hundred struggle sessions – including one in front of 10,000 people at the Workers Stadium – before dying in prison in 1969.

One professor victimised in the Cultural Revolution later commented on how many Red Guards shouted the slogan 'revolution is not a crime', revealing some deeper awareness that what they were doing was wrong.[16] When the 62-year-old feminist author Ding Ling was forced into in the 'airplane' stress position, bent at the waist while Red Guards beat and abused her, she was on the verge of passing out when one of them suddenly commanded, 'Stand up straight and let the masses see your face!'[17] Ding Ling later recalled this as a discreet act of compassion.

'Revolution is not a crime'

There was no sign of compassion, remorse or hesitation among the mob of Red Guards who, on a broiling August afternoon, dragged nearly thirty other prominent writers, scholars and opera stars to the Pavilion of Exalted Literature at the dynastic-era imperial college near Beijing's Lama Temple. After shaving their victims' heads, they forced them to kneel for hours, heads pressed to the hot paving stones before a bonfire of books and Peking Opera costumes. They screamed abuse at them while whipping them with belt buckles and striking them with bamboo rods and Peking Opera props.

32

Among their victims was one of China's most well-loved novelists and playwrights, Lao She (a pen name). The author of iconic works such as the novel *Rickshaw Boy* and the play *Teahouse*, Lao She had been the first cultural figure to be named a People's Artist after the founding of the People's Republic. At 67, he was chairman of the Beijing Writers' Association and vice-chairman of the Chinese Writers' Association – a solid member of the cultural establishment now accused of promoting an 'anti-Party, anti-socialist revisionist line'. He had once urged other 'gentle people' like himself to 'cast off your sentimentality and refinement... extend your fist, open your eyes....' This time, the fists were raised against him.

At the end of the afternoon, the Red Guards took a bruised and bloodied Lao She back to the Writers' Association office, where they beat him some more as his colleagues either looked on silently or joined in the abuse. The Red Guards ordered him to return the following day for more 'criticism'. Arriving home later that night, he found his house ransacked, his art collection destroyed and his manuscripts shredded.

When Red Guards came looking for him the next day, he had disappeared. His body was discovered in one of the capital's artificial lakes, his pockets full of stones. The crematorium workers threw away his ashes.

The many cultural figures who committed suicide following abuse by Red Guards included orchestra conductors, opera singers, writers and translators. Nearly 18 percent of 'unnatural deaths' in Beijing alone between 1966 and 1976 are believed to have been suicides.[18]

Among other prominent cultural figures targeted and abused by Red Guards was the author of the Chinese national anthem, *March of the Volunteers*, Tian Han. Tian died in prison, an alleged 'counter-revolutionary'.

Unnatural deaths

* * *

Foreign connections were automatically suspect. Yang Xianyi was the urbane, Oxford-educated son of a Tianjin banker who'd returned from England in 1940 with his China-born English wife, Gladys Tayler Yang, to join the revolutionary underground. In 1966, they worked as translators in the Foreign Languages Bureau, where they also lived with their three

33

children. They were working on an English translation of an eighteenth-century literary masterpiece when the order came down for work on all translations to stop. Yang sensed 'the axe was about to fall'.

Big-character posters denouncing revisionists, spies and traitors soon covered the office walls. For days, Yang listened to loudspeakers blaring denunciations of colleagues, who were then dragged off to be 'struggled'. He wrote in his memoir *White Tiger* that he'd managed to keep his nerve in pre-revolutionary times, once when Chiang Kai-shek's soldiers aimed their rifles at him and on another occasion on a sinking boat. This felt scarier. Soon enough, a slew of *dàzìbào* went up denouncing him as a reactionary revisionist and 'Khrushchev's grandson'.

In the compound's dining hall, Red Guards forced him into the airplane stress position atop three precariously stacked tables and accused him of being anti-Mao. Terrified that they intended to murder him, he appealed for someone to contact a government minister he knew – unaware that the man had also come under attack and had already committed suicide.

Some foreigners among the bureau's non-Chinese editors and translators supported the Red Guards. Israel Epstein had arrived in Tianjin in 1917 as the two-year-old son of socialist Polish refugees. In his twenties he covered the Japanese invasion of China for Western media, making his way to the Communist stronghold of Yan'an in 1944, where conversations with Mao inspired him to devote his life to the communist cause. After the revolution, he edited the English-language *China Reconstructs*, aimed at readers abroad. He became a Chinese citizen in 1957 and in 1964 joined the Party. Enthusiastically welcoming the onset of the Cultural Revolution, he helped to form a rebel regiment that included fellow 'foreign experts' from Chile, Belgium and Sri Lanka.

Other 'foreign friends' on the side of the rebels included the American Sidney Rittenberg, a left-wing university activist who had trained in the Chinese language after being drafted into the US Army. Like Epstein, Rittenberg met Mao and the other leaders in Yan'an and later joined the Chinese

Foreign friends

34

Communist Party. He worked for Xinhua News Agency and Radio Peking and, along with Epstein, was part of the team that translated the Fourth Volume of the *Selected Works of Mao Zedong* into English. Rittenberg threw himself into the Cultural Revolution, even leading rebels to take over the state broadcaster. He had reportedly pointed the Red Guards at Xianyi and Gladys Yang.[19]

Linking Up

At the end of August, the Party urged Beijing students – the Red Guard vanguard – to travel around the country in a great 'exchange of revolutionary experience' known as *chuānlián*, or 'linking up'. The Party made train and bus tickets free for them and ordered local authorities to provide them with accommodation – typically straw or bamboo mats on the floor of a school classroom or gym. It was a great adventure. Few Chinese at the time had the opportunity to travel even in their own country, and especially unsupervised.

Spreading the revolution across the country

Packing the trains and buses well beyond the limits of safety and basic sanitation, Red Guards inadvertently sparked an epidemic of cerebrospinal meningitis that eventually killed 160,000 people around the country. Their monopolising of public transport had economic consequences as well, leading some Party leaders to suggest the 'New Long Marchers' model themselves on the heroes of the original Long March and travel by foot. Various localities hosted receptions for those who did, with banners reading 'Long live the Long March Spirit!'

On their travels, the students visited revolutionary 'sacred sites' like Yan'an and various model communes and participated in local struggle sessions. In one area of southwestern Guangxi province alone, local and visiting Red Guards 'struggled' nearly 12,000 primary and high school teachers, killing 206 of them and leaving 108 permanently disabled.[20]

Red Guards also targeted landlords and capitalists. The problem was, there weren't many of either category left. Seventeen years of communist rule had included the state takeover of most businesses and the communalisation of almost all property in the 1950s. One Red Guard assigned to watch Nien Cheng confided that his family was also under attack.

Although they'd been workers for generations, his aunt's fruit stall had suddenly made her a 'capitalist'.

Former landholders, whether living off savings in cities or as peasants on their old family land, were now fair game. So too were former business owners, even those who were now workers in factories they'd once owned.

In addition to teachers, pretty much any older person with an education was a target. In the revolutionary argot of the time, 'intellectuals' were members of the 'Stinking Ninth Category' – language borrowed from the Mongol Yuan dynasty (1271–1368), which divided its Chinese subjects into a hierarchy of ten groups; only beggars rated lower than scholars. Anyone who had been targeted in a previous thought reform or 'rectification' campaign going back to the 1940s could be victimised as well.

The fury with which many locals collaborated with Red Guards in attacking local officials derived from years of grudges and resentment at their privileges, including during the famine. As one person put it, 'We starve until our skulls shine through our scalps, while the cadres glisten with fat'.[21]

In November 1966, Beijing Red Guards arrived in Qufu, Shandong province, where Confucius, who preached moderation, stability, hierarchy and the importance of scholarship, had been born in 551 BCE. They joined up with local Red Guards to ransack the sage's ancestral home, parade his toppled statue through the town and 'struggle' experts in his teachings. In 29 days of Red Guard activity there, they destroyed some 100,000 volumes of classical texts, including 1,700 rare items, damaged 6,618 cultural artefacts, smashed 1,000 carved stone stelae and cut down 5,000 ancient pines. They also dynamited Confucius's tomb and dug up half a dozen of his descendants' graves, watched by thousands of curious onlookers. The discovery of gold and other precious objects in some of them – duly handed over to members of the local Cultural Relics Committee and People's Bank – set off 'something of a grave-robbing mania' in the area, culminating in the excavation of some 2,000 of his descendants' remains over the following year.[22]

* * *

As the radical students emptied the classrooms to jump on the trains, the teachers and administrators left behind read the newspapers, studied Mao's writings or, if they were being punished, cleaned toilets or shovelled coal. Many of the students who stayed behind took up hobbies such as knitting or electronics, read, learned languages or practiced calligraphy. One who spent his time studying ancient oracle bone script would later become a recognised expert. It was, paradoxically, an age of great freedom for both the young people travelling around the country to spread revolution as well as many of those left behind.

The Two Faces of Zhou Enlai

Zhou Enlai: 'What other nation in the world possesses so much freedom?'

Suave, handsome, well-spoken and worldly, Zhou Enlai came from a clan that had produced many Qing dynasty officials and scholars but had since fallen on hard times. A capable and diligent student, he'd attracted sponsorship for study in Japan and later France, where he joined the Communist Party. After 1949, he became the first premier and foreign minister of the

People's Republic, serving as its charming and charismatic face to the world.

Zhou protected certain cultural treasures and historic sites from destruction. These included the Forbidden City, the Jade Buddha Temple in Shanghai and Potala Palace in Tibet. He also let countless others be obliterated. He famously kept some people safe, such as former vice-president Song Qingling, who had broken with her wealthy and prominent Shanghainese family to support the communists before the revolution, as well as a night-soil collector who'd enjoyed the privilege of being singled out as a model labourer by Liu Shaoqi before the president himself fell from grace. Yet Zhou also infamously authorised the persecution of people he knew did not deserve it, including his own stepdaughter and brother. He never broke ranks with Mao, endorsing the Cultural Revolution as a 'fierce and long-term struggle' vital to the country's future and declaring that 'we must never – *never* – pour cold water on the young'.[23]

In September, Zhou himself came under attack. The Red Guards, fed up with his attempts at moderation, called him a 'double-dealer playing with counter-revolution' and an 'insincere opportunist'. Posters reading 'Bombard Zhou Enlai!' appeared in the Foreign Language Institute. The unflappable premier went for a long walk with a group of antagonistic Red Guards on a late September night, only parting in the early hours of the following morning. He told them that the 'Bombard Zhou Enlai' poster didn't bother him. He celebrated their ability to say such things: 'What other nation in the world possesses so much freedom?' Still, he suggested that maybe they shouldn't actually kill people.

Zhou performed a number of ostentatious acts of humility, for example tucking the quilts around the feet of soldiers who'd come to Beijing for the 1 October National Day celebrations and were staying in a hostel within the Zhongnanhai leadership compound. When waiters at the Peking Hotel declared that they'd no longer polish the shoes of guests, Zhou offered to do it himself.

As premier and person in charge of the apparatus of state, Zhou tried to keep the wheels of the government and

Zhou's common touch

38

economy from falling off. In November, after workers began leaving their posts around the country to make Red Guard-like pilgrimages to the revolutionary centre of Beijing, Zhou Enlai tried to limit their numbers. The capital didn't have the resources to receive them all, and production couldn't be allowed to suffer. At the same time, Zhou instructed factory managers not to punish workers who insisted on going. When Lin Biao told Red Guards to go after revisionists and counter-revolutionaries in government positions, Zhou Enlai reportedly glowered.

No One is Safe

Mao had frequently praised Tao Zhu, a former Party secretary of Guangdong province, as being 'premier material'. In May he promoted him to the fourth most powerful position in the leadership, after himself, Lin Biao and Zhou Enlai. In August 1966, Tao joined the Politburo Standing Committee and was made director of the Central Propaganda Department. He had supported the launch of the Cultural Revolution but balked at some of its excesses.

In September 1966, Tao Zhu heard a rumour that Liu Shaoqi and Deng Xiaoping were to be 'pulled off their horses'. He found it hard to credit. He reportedly told his wife that, even if they'd made mistakes, Liu was still the president and Deng Snakes and ladders a member of the Politburo Standing Committee. So when he learned that state media were planning to omit Liu and Deng from the official photos of the 1 October National Day celebrations, he ordered them reinstated 'as per the rules'.[24]

Later that month at a Party meeting, Mao acknowledged that the Great Cultural Revolution had 'wreaked havoc' following the publication of 'Bombard the Headquarters'. He said that he had not foreseen such nationwide turmoil. But he had no plans to stop it, either.

Lin Biao described the violence as a 'dynamic mopping up and elimination operation' that was necessary to lay a 'solid foundation' for the new culture they would create once the old one was destroyed. It could take decades to accomplish, Lin said, but he exhorted his fellow leaders 'not to fear chaos', to keep faith in Mao and the Party and to trust the masses.

At the same meeting, Liu Shaoqi criticised himself for numerous 'errors' dating back to 1945. These included 'distrusting the masses' in his handling of the campus work teams back in June. Mao conceded that however grievous were the errors of Liu Shaoqi and Deng Xiaoping, they had 'always done their work in the open, not in secret'. In other words, they were not underhanded conspirators like former Beijing mayor Peng Zhen: 'People should be allowed to make some mistakes.' Yet he also demanded an intense struggle against the pair's 'bourgeois reactionary line'. Liu made a nervous, morose figure at subsequent official events, including the last Red Guard rallies in November, disappearing altogether from public view after 11 December.

Two-line struggle   As the 'two-line struggle' between Mao and Liu became public, revolutionary activists, including Red Guards, began to split into hostile 'rebel' and 'conservative' factions.

A Toast to All-Out Civil War
Mao turned 73 on 26 December 1966. Close associates gathered for a meal at his poolside residence in the official leadership compound of Zhongnanhai in the old Imperial City. Invitees included the head of his personal bodyguard, Wang Dongxing, and members of the Central Cultural Revolution Group. One of those was Qi Benyu, a Party theorist, propagandist, Mao's secretary since May and an aide to Jiang Qing. In his memoirs, Qi described a banquet of braised pork, stewed fish, bacon with garlic shoots, tofu, 'long-life noodles' and other dishes.

Mao reflected on the 'excellent' chaos in Shanghai, where tens of thousands of rebels from different factions had recently brawled in the streets. Enumerating some of the year's other highlights – including the 16 May Circular and the Red Guard linkups – he said, 'we're not done yet.' Raising a cup of warm rice wine, he made a toast to 'all-out civil war and next year's victory'. Qi Benyu said the idea of 'all-out civil war' took everybody by surprise, even though they hid it well.[25]

40

PART THREE

1967–69: Violence, Confusion and Contradiction

Classes struggle, some classes triumph, others
are extinguished. Such is history.

Mao Zedong

The all-important 1 January editorial in the *People's Daily*
heralded a year of 'nationwide, full-scale class struggle'. If
'struggle' in 1966 had individuals as its object in 1967 the focus
would turn to eliminating entire classes of people, as it
spread from the cities to the wider countryside. The first
mass murder of members of the Five Black Categories took
place in September 1966 in Daxing County on Beijing's outskirts. The leaders of the area's thirteen communes authorised the extermination of all landlords, 'rightists' and other
enemies of the people along with their families. In an orgy of
violence, radical cadres, activists and local militias beat,   First mass murder
stabbed and strangled to death 325 adults and children, including a one-month-old baby.

Yu Luoke was a young man who had spent some time
working on farms in Daxing. Although he'd graduated from
high school in 1959 at the top of his class, he wasn't admitted to university because his parents had been deemed to be
rightists two years earlier. In 1964, he returned from Daxing
to Beijing to work as a sessional teacher but lost his job two
years later after writing an essay in defence of Wu Han.

Yu's contacts in Daxing told him about the massacre there.
He wrote a powerful essay in response, 'On Class Origins',
that used both Maoist and Marxist theory in a devastating
critique of the Bloodlines Theory. Victimising the Five Black
Categories, he argued, 'chilled the enthusiasm for revolution'

41

of countless youth. All young people in 1966, whatever their family background, had been raised socialist. Not all people of 'good class background' did good things; the theory was a 'recipe for misrule'. Besides, if Mao Zedong Thought was an 'invincible ideological weapon', why did it not prevail over the happenstance of family background?[26]

'On Class Origins' published

Yu Luoke printed copies of his essay in January 1967 and sold them for two Chinese cents, eventually distributing over 100,000 copies nationwide. Popularly produced publications were not unusual in that era – Red Guards published anywhere between three and ten thousand newsletters between 1966 and 1968 alone.[27]

So many people wrote grateful letters to Yu in response that the post office couldn't physically deliver them all.[28] Four months after its publication, the authorities would declare 'On Class Origins' a 'poisonous weed' and shut down the journal he and his brother had created to publish it. By then it had an editorial board of twenty people that also organised debates and seminars.

Security forces would eventually arrest Yu Luoke and charge him with making 'counter-revolutionary propaganda' and organising 'counter-revolutionary cliques'. On 5 March, 1970, at the age of twenty-seven, he would be put on public trial at the Workers Stadium in Beijing in front of tens of thousands of jeering onlookers and then executed.

For now, though, the Party let him be. They had more pressing things on their minds. The Party itself was ambivalent about the 'Bloodlines' debate. Jiang Qing had denounced it and leading Party journals now published an article characterising it as a reactionary plot to sow division among radical students. But that was for the Party to decide.

Workers Unite, Local Governments Fall

Zhou Enlai's attempts to keep the Cultural Revolution from spilling into offices and factories had failed. By early 1967, workers had thrown themselves into the fray. Their involvement worried the Party, especially when they spoke of striking for better wages and entitlements, a prospect from which even the most radical Communist Party leaders recoiled.

42

Nowhere were workers more fully invested in making revolution than in the industrial hub of Shanghai. In November, after local authorities refused them permission to form a city-wide rebel group, about a thousand workers commandeered a train headed north to Beijing to complain. Stopped at Anting, outside Shanghai, they refused to disembark, blocking Shanghai–Beijing rail traffic for nearly two days. Their leader, Wang Hongwen, would rise to become one of Jiang Qing's 'Gang of Four'. After the Cultural Revolution Group negotiated a truce, other workers around the country demanded the right to rebel as well.

Rebel groups marching in Shanghai in 1967

On 6 January 1967, Shanghai workers staged an epic struggle session in the People's Square against members of the Shanghai Municipal Committee and local Party functionaries, including the mayor, whose reign they declared over. Hundreds of thousands of people attended the main and ancillary struggle sessions.

On 11 January, the Party Centre congratulated the rebels on seizing power, sparking a nationwide movement among radical 'mass organisations' to overthrow local and regional governments. Mao had ordained a civil war but he had no grand plan for how it would unfold. As he wrote in 'On Practice', first comes the experience, then you work out the theory.

On 5 February in Shanghai, workers declared the establishment of the New Shanghai People's Commune, its name a homage to the revolutionary Paris Commune of 1871. Hundreds of thousands of people flooded into the streets waving red flags and revolutionary placards in support. Zhang Chunqiao and Yao Wenyuan of the Central Cultural Revolution Leading Group were actively involved with the communards.

The leaders of the Shanghai Commune proposed eliminating all power hierarchies and introducing universal suffrage. This would effectively deny the Communist Party its role as the revolutionary vanguard, the basis of its rule. One Red Guard publication proclaimed that radicals everywhere were 'clapping their hands with joy' at the thought of similar communes throughout the country.[29] Mao was not applauding. He recalled Zhang Chunqiao and Yao Wenyuan to the capital and told them that universal democracy was a 'most reactionary' idea. Mao, forever balancing his twin desires for destruction and construction, needed to preserve some form of Party-led government.

The Shanghai Commune folded after eighteen days of power struggles and disorder, including four days when the city's 6.4 million people had neither water nor electricity. After the commune's collapse, a committee consisting of a 'three-way alliance' of military personnel, Party cadres and representatives of the 'revolutionary masses' took over. Revolutionary committees based on this three-way alliance became the new model for local administration.

Enter the Army

Mao had Lin Biao order the army to quell the surging factional violence and help 'support the leftist masses' to take power. The idea that the army should make political judgements, such as determining which of the competing Red Guard and other groups were most 'left', disquieted a number of Party elders, including some generals. Heated arguments broke out between veteran commanders and members of the Cultural Revolution Group over the role of the army in the Cultural Revolution and the radical course it was taking.

Eventually Mao stepped in on the side of the radicals,

repeating his 1958 threat that he would raise a guerrilla force and lead an insurgency if he didn't get his way. The generals gave in. The radicals were triumphant. Mao cancelled future meetings of the Politburo. By the standards of the day, however, the punishments meted out to those associated with what was now labelled the 'February Countercurrent' were not severe. What's more, Mao lambasted the Cultural Revolution Leading Group for acting like an 'independent kingdom' and told Jiang Qing to criticise herself for her 'high aspirations but low capacity'. No one ever knew exactly where they stood with Mao. This was one source of his power.

The army's involvement in the Cultural Revolution ramped up the levels of violence. In the street battles of 1966, Red Guard factions had mostly used improvised weapons: iron fenceposts sharpened into spears and makeshift catapults made from bicycle tires and bricks. In 1967, some 19 million guns, nearly 15,000 heavy artillery and almost 3 million grenades would fall into the hands of students, workers and other civilian rebels. Some were given the weapons by the army. Others fought army units for them or simply stole them.

* * *

Reflecting the simmering divisions within the top leadership, the Party continued to issue mixed signals. On 23 February, it put the brakes on free train travel to encourage young people to stay at school – while telling everyone to keep making revolution. Conflicting policies and directives only energised the toxic quarrels among the 'revolutionary masses'.

The Higher You Climb...

In early 1967, radical workers at the leadership compound in Zhongnanhai surrounded 'the capitalist roader' Liu Shaoqi's villa and cut the president's phone lines. Tao Zhu also became a target. 'Overthrow Liu, Deng and Tao!' entered the growing lexicon of popular slogans.

In January, Red Guards unfurled 15-metre banners around Tiananmen Square calling for Zhou Enlai to be burnt alive. This proved a step too far – a 'counter-revolutionary act' according to the security chief Kang Sheng. Although anti-Zhou sentiment continued to simmer within Jiang Qing's radical coterie in particular, Mao read them the riot act over their attacks on Zhou.

Others in the political elite were not so lucky. Under Kang Sheng's direction, interrogators deprived high-ranking victims of sleep, isolated and beat them, refused them medical treatment and fed them starvation rations. Red Guard groups could formally apply to 'borrow' the prisoners for struggle sessions so long as they handed them back more or less alive afterwards. Regional 'Investigation Groups' followed similar protocols. In all, some two million leading cadres would be subjected to 'investigation'.[30]

The families of victims, from high-ranking officials to ordinary 'cow demons and snake spirits', suffered too. The half-sister of Xi Jinping, later leader of the Party from 2012 onwards, committed suicide after Red Guards ransacked their home. Deng Pufang, the son of Deng Xiaoping, either fell, jumped or was pushed from a three-storey building on the Peking University campus in 1968 while under interrogation by Red Guards; he broke his back and would be confined to a wheelchair for the rest of his life.

Wang Guangmei, wife of Liu Shaoqi, is humiliated in public in a costume parodying her 'bourgeois' style, including her *cheongsam* and pearls.

In some cases, the children of victims joined in the attacks or helped to set them up. Liu Shaoqi's daughter Liu Tao lured her stepmother Wang Guangmei out of the heavily guarded Zhongnanhai compound. This allowed Kuai Dafu, the charismatic son of a poor peasant who led a major Tsinghua University Red Guard group, to kidnap her. Although Wang initially outwitted the Red Guards, several months later they demanded she appear at a mass struggle session on the Tsinghua University campus. Mao and Zhou both ordered her to go. Hundreds of thousands of people bayed for her blood as she shivered in an excessively tight summer *cheongsam* and a 'pearl necklace' of ping pong balls, an outfit parodying her 'bourgeois' style when she had travelled overseas as a diplomatic envoy for the PRC. Jiang Qing told the Red Guards to dress her like that; Wang Guangmei was one of many veteran women revolutionaries against whom she held a grudge.[31]

The many grudges of Jiang Qing

Jiang Qing was a complex character, a fierce ideologue and rabble-rousing orator, prone to fits of pique, yet humble before Mao and able to impress a visiting Imelda Marcos several years later with her 'femininity' and soft-spokenness. In the early 1970s, she would pose for her American biographer Roxane Witke's camera in a 'luminous' silk dress as she pressed orchids while seated in a traditional pavilion near a lotus pond where songbirds chirped in their cages. An ordinary woman might have been struggled to within an inch of her life for such 'bourgeois' style. Wang Guangmei certainly was. Like her husband, Jiang Qing played by different rules.

* * *

Nonstop violence and pervasive fear took its toll on people's mental health. Following multiple struggle sessions in Beijing's Foreign Languages Bureau, Yang Xianyi suffered from terrifying auditory hallucinations. One day he heard a colleague being interrogated and beaten to death, only to run into him at lunch very much alive.

Putting the Cult in Cultural Revolution

The spring of 1967 saw the full flourishing of Mao's personality cult. Larger-than-life statues of the Great Helmsman sprang up on campuses and in public squares. Every home and workplace acquired at least one Mao portrait, to which people bowed ritualistically in the morning to 'ask for instructions' and again at night to 'report back'.

Young people performed flash-mob-style 'Loyalty Dances'

while singing adulatory songs with titles like 'Sailing the Seas Depends on the Helmsman', 'Beloved Chairman Mao' and 'If You Don't Beat Them, They'll Never be Overthrown'.[32] They compared themselves to sunflowers turning their faces to Mao, the Red Sun.

Billboards, banners and slogans proclaimed Mao's wisdom on streets and farms and in schools and factories. Flight attendants led those privileged enough to fly in the recitation of quotations and singalongs on the journey. 'It is because our Party and people have a helmsman of such genius as Comrade Mao Zedong and the great thought of Mao Zedong is the compass to chart the correct course through heavy fog,' the *People's Daily* declared in a state of metaphorical overdrive, that 'the great ship of our revolution has been able to steer clear of the countless dangerous shoals and hidden rocks and, in the teeth of great storms and waves, sail victoriously along the revolutionary course of Marxism Leninism'.

The Great Helmsman

The propaganda machinery wheeled out a pantheon of model workers, peasants, cadres and soldiers, including Lei Feng, who shared the defining quality of a selfless devotion to Mao. There was even a model 'internationalist' as well, the Canadian doctor Norman Bethune, who died of an infection in 1939 while serving with the Communist forces in the war of resistance against the Japanese occupation. Mao's essay in memory of Bethune became a canonical text of the Cultural Revolution alongside 'Serve the People'.

The Cultural Revolution produced a rich and colourful iconography, available as merch. Everyone wore at least one 'Mao Badge'. Some 2.5 billion badges were produced in more than 20,000 designs over a ten-year-period. Some were as big as plates, others tiny, while some even glowed in the dark. Thinking of the wasted metal, Mao is said to have remarked, 'Give back our planes.'

Mao badges

He might have asked for his forests back as well. In 1962, Mao's writings comprised only 0.5 percent of all published titles. By June 1966 they represented 'basically the whole Chinese publishing industry'.[33] By the end of 1967, China's publishing houses had printed some 350 million copies of the Little Red Book (a state-subsidised bargain at RMB2) and 80 million

48

copies of the then four-volume set of his selected work. These, along with his collected poems, a set of photographs and another of his publications were known as the 'five precious gifts'. Royalties made Mao the richest person in China.[34]

As traditionally was the case with Buddhist statuary or scripture, you didn't 'buy' (mǎi) Mao badges, posters, busts or books. You 'invited' (qǐng) them into your home. (You still had to pay for them.) Accidentally defacing a newspaper that contained Mao's words or photo was an act of heresy that could get a person imprisoned, a tough call at a time when his words and pictures were all over the press, and a lack of alternatives meant newspapers frequently did second service as rubbish wrappers, toilet paper, cigarette paper and even menstrual pads.

By the end of May, the arias from Jiang Qing's revolutionary model operas, praised by the *People's Daily* as 'holding high the great red banner of Mao Zedong Thought', could be heard everywhere.

Any form of resistance had to be subtle to the point of imperceptibility and deniability. In Tibet, where the traditional sign of respect was to touch one's head to a deity's image, some slept with their feet facing Mao's portrait.

Coded dissent

Mao Gets His Civil War

By the end of February, the army had worked with some radical groups to establish 'three-way alliance' Revolutionary Committees in Shanghai, Shandong and Guizhou. Elsewhere, things got messy. A major problem was that many army units enjoyed longstanding, amicable relationships with established Party and government authorities in the regions where they were stationed. Defying orders, some chose to support these local authorities against the radical groups now trying to overthrow them.

In January 1967, in the city of Shihezi in northwestern Xinjiang, an army regiment aligned with the local Party committee opened fire on local radicals with automatic weapons, killing 26 people and wounding 74. It was the year's first massacre of citizens by the army. The second occurred the following month in Xining, the capital of Qinghai province.

Guizhou, 1967. The banner in the center reads: 'The People's Liberation Army firmly supports the proletarian revolutionary faction.'

Rebels trying to overthrow the local government had occupied the *Qinghai Daily* offices. Their supporters kept watch outside in the newspaper's compound, huddling around campfires against the bitter cold and singing revolutionary songs. They refused the army's repeated orders to leave, even throwing a soldier who'd entered the compound back over the wall.

On the morning of 23 February, soldiers stormed the compound, machine guns blazing, leaving 169 civilian corpses scattered on the blood-soaked snow.[35] They mercilessly beat the surviving rebels – old, young, women, men, editors, journalists, workers, students, ordinary citizens alike. More than 13,000 people were arrested and 4,000 sent to labour camps.

50

Factional warfare was one major type of violence in 1967. Another was mass killings of 'class enemies' by radical local authorities and militias. As with the massacre in Daxing County the previous year, pogroms targeting members of the Five Black Categories and other 'class enemies' were carefully organised events. Local officials held meetings beforehand to discuss tactics and draw up lists of people to murder.[36]

In August 1967, Party officials in Dao county, Hunan province, decided to cleanse their area completely of the Five Black Categories, slaughtering somewhere between 4,500 and 9,000 people, including children and the elderly. Some were clubbed to death, others packed into cellars to suffocate and still others bound in groups around sticks of dynamite and blown up. So many bodies were thrown into limestone pits to dissolve that there is no definitive death toll. One of the eager participants in the slaughter was an illiterate, bad-tempered ne'er-do-well who stabbed seven 'class enemies' to death and then, in a state of high excitement, went hunting for more, killing a pair of toddlers at the house of a landowner. The local authorities awarded him 55 *yuan*, more than he had ever earned in a year.

The killing escalates

Academics estimate that between 500,000 and 2 million 'excess deaths' took place in the Chinese countryside over the course of the Cultural Revolution, many of them in 1967. Guangdong and Guangxi provinces were among the worst affected, with the highest death rate in the country (nearly two out of every thousand people). Official media continued to issue mixed signals, admonishing the rebels to forge a 'great unity' on the one hand while urging them to 'hound the enemies to the end' on the other.[37]

Across the nation, the scale and intensity of conflict was escalating. In Chongqing, where the PLA supported the local government, officials encouraged the city's workers and peasants to 'imprison, beat and torture' the rebels trying to overthrow them.[38] The army helpfully provided their allies with machine guns, napalm, tanks and even warships. The death toll there rose to over one thousand. More than 10,000 people fled the city for the hinterland. The combatants regularly executed their captives, including pregnant women and the

51

wounded. As the documentarian Wang Youqin has written, 'the rules of the Cultural Revolution were harsher than war.'

In Guangxi province, which borders Vietnam, rebels armed themselves with weapons stolen from shipments intended for the Viet Cong, including anti-tank and anti-aircraft guns. One battle reduced the city of Wuzhou to rubble; another flattened whole areas of Nanning, the provincial capital.

The Wuhan Counter-Revolutionary Incident[39]

Wuhan, the capital of Hebei province, was another hot spot. Between January and July 1967, two warring factions waged more than three hundred skirmishes on its streets, some involving tens of thousands of combatants and heavy artillery. On one side was a group calling itself the Workers' General Headquarters. This was an alliance of workers and the most radical Red Guards determined to overthrow the municipal government and replace it with a 'three-way' revolutionary committee. Supporting the municipal government was a military faction called the Million Heroes, soldiers fiercely loyal to their commander, Chen Zaidao. Each side claimed about half a million supporters.

The leadership in Beijing was worried. Wuhan was a crucial centre for heavy industry, a Yangtze port and a vital north–south transport hub. The fighting was disrupting freight and transport as well as production at the area's 2,400 mines and factories.

On 13 July, Mao told the other leaders that he planned to wind up the Cultural Revolution by the end of 1968. He also wanted to go to Wuhan for another swim in the Yangtze. The others were flabbergasted, worried both for their impulsive Chairman's safety and for their own should he meet misadventure. They told him that Wuhan was too chaotic. There were plenty of other great places to swim; they even suggested a few. But Mao insisted. He wasn't afraid of chaos. The group hurriedly decided that Yang Chengwu, Mao's acting chief of staff, would accompany him and that Premier Zhou Enlai would fly down in advance.

An outing to Wuhan

Two Party emissaries, meanwhile, arrived in Wuhan to try to negotiate a peace between the two warring sides first.

They had already been to several other provinces on similar missions. One of the envoys was Vice Premier Xie Fuzhi, who as public security minister had ordered police not to intervene in Red Guard violence. The other was Wang Li, a member of the Cultural Revolution Leading Group. Mao arrived later that evening on his special train. Despite his lack of concern, his guards secured the train station and put gunboats, planes and helicopters on standby for any emergency.

On 18 July, Mao met with Chen Zaidao, the regional PLA commander who led the Million Heroes. Chen had been a young orphaned cowherd when he joined the Party. The army had been his family ever since. Mao reassured Chen that he wasn't in too much trouble, but the two sides needed to meet and resolve their differences; after all, both were fighting in his name.

Zhou was already flying back to Beijing when Xie Fuzhi and Wang Li, without authorisation, assured some Red Guards in the Workers General Headquarters that their side had the 'unwavering support' of Mao, Lin Biao and the Cultural Revolution Leading Group. They were being recorded. The following day, 19 July, the Red Guards broadcast the emissaries' words on every street in Wuhan and from every bridge and dock. The Million Heroes reacted with fury. Hundreds of trucks packed with armed soldiers and workers roared through the streets, followed by thousands more vehicles carrying workers, peasants and other sympathisers.

Two hundred members of the Million Heroes charged the emissaries' guesthouse, sealing off the area and mounting machine guns on the surrounding roofs. They had no idea that Mao, whose visit had been kept secret, was also in residence. When news of the unfolding events reached Lin Biao, Jiang Qing and others in Beijing, they dispatched a plane to rescue Mao, urging him to leave immediately, saying his life was in danger.

Zhou also returned to Wuhan, though his own plane had to divert to another, secondary airport to avoid a kidnapping plot. He finally made it to the villa where Mao was staying but had a hard time convincing the Chairman – who among other things, hated flying – to leave with him by plane.

Mao plunges into the chaos

After Mao reluctantly agreed, they smuggled him in convoy through the streets of Wuhan in the dead of night to the airport. It was the last flight he would ever take. Once in Shanghai, Mao told his chief of staff Yang Chengwu that given that Chen Zaidao had let him leave the city, he couldn't be as bad as everyone said.

The night of Mao's escape, the Million Heroes viciously beat Xie and Wang, tearing out clumps of Wang's hair and leaving him with a bruised face and swollen eye; they also reportedly killed Xie's secretary. Zhou Enlai rescued the pair a few days later and flew them back to the capital, where Jiang Qing and Lin Biao had organised tens of thousands of people to be at the airport to cheer their return. Declaring the incident the result of 'counter-revolutionary turmoil', Lin Biao relieved Chen Zaidao of his position. Although Mao continued to insist Chen was a 'comrade' who should make a self-criticism, and not an enemy to be punished, the incident did seem to cool his enthusiasm for mass movements.

* * *

Beijing students prepare big-character posters denouncing Liu Shaoqi, 1967.

On 26 July, Cultural Revolution Group member Qi Benyu told the Red Guard leader Kuai Dafu that overthrowing the 'capitalist roader' and 'traitor' Liu Shaoqi was now a matter of urgent importance. Kuai led 200,000 Red Guards to camp outside Zhongnanhai in what they called a *jiū Liú huŏxiàn*, or

The official face of the Cultural Revolution: mobilised, united and in thrall. Clockwise from above: teenagers perform revolution for the 'masses', young men take inspiration from Mao's writings before plunging into the Yangtze to commemorate his heroic swim a year earlier, and (left) workers thrill at a preserved mango, Mao's gift to his new revolutionary vanguard.

千钧霹雳开新宇──炮打司令部

Propaganda posters transformed Mao's pencil jottings into a mighty wielding of brush and ink, while heroic choreography obscured a messy reality.

On your guard: At a mass rally, Mao suggested to Red Guard Song Binbin, whose name means gentle or refined, that she change it to '*yàowǔ*', meaning 'be militant'. Primed for revolutionary action and believing enemies of the revolution to be lurking everywhere, Red Guards targeted those closest to hand: their teachers and principals. Many of the early victims of Red Guard 'struggle sessions' and violence were educators, including the high school teacher murdered by the group surrounding Song Binbin. The sign around the neck of the man portrayed in the statuette (right) identifies him as a 'reactionary academic authority'.

The cult in train: The poster of a youthful Mao on the road to Anyuan (left) became one of the era's most iconic images, along with the ubiquitous Mao badges (example below). An endless stream of propaganda images rapidly turned him into a godlike figure.

All the world's a stage: While Red Guards were busy destroying China's old culture, Mao's wife Jiang Qing led the construction of a new one. A former actor in Shanghai, Jiang (pictured left in 1935) had led a double life as a member of the Communist underground. Formulaic, heroic and stirring, the 'revolutionary model operas' she devised – which included ballets, symphonies and other stage productions – dominated China's theatres and public squares for a decade. During US President Nixon's pathbreaking visit to China, Jiang Qing invited him to see the *Red Detachment of Women* (below). The Nixons were confounded by her statement that the ballet had been authored by 'the masses'.

Historical reflux: Images from the Cultural Revolution can inspire a kind of amnesiac nostalgia. But in 1989, when students and their supporters filled the square once thronged by Red Guards, this time holding banners demanding democracy and a free press, they were met with tanks. One anonymous citizen provided the most enduring image of the Tiananmen Square protests when he stood in their way.

'Grab Liu Action Front'. Through three weeks of heavy rain, cold nights and steamy hot days, they flew their banners and shouted for Liu's surrender through loudhailers. The leadership had to plead for a few hours of silence at night to sleep.

The mob also intended to kidnap Zhou Enlai should he appear to negotiate. When it was clear neither Liu nor Zhou would come out, the Red Guards fought one another for a while and then dispersed.

The radicals at the top then gave Kuai Dafu a new task: gathering intelligence on other 'capitalist-road commanders' like Chen Zaidao and their followers in the military to prevent another Wuhan-style incident. With the righteousness and urgency of a Red Army general in the propaganda films his generation had grown up on, Kuai pored over military maps and cabled Red Guard leaders around the country. After Red Guards raided the home of a vice-chairman of the military commission, seizing seven safes full of classified material, the Central Committee ordered the Beijing Garrison to reclaim the secret documents. Before they could do so, Kuai and his allies hand-copied everything they could, dispersing confidential military secrets across the land.[40] Among these allies were members of another major Red Guard organisation led by Nie Yuanzi, the author of the big-character poster that inspired Mao's 'Bombard the Headquarters'.

Back in Wuhan, 'Comrade' Chen Zaidao's Million Heroes and their civilian supporters swarmed the campuses, set fire to schools and hunted down Red Guards. In response, Lin Biao ordered PLA units loyal to him to eradicate them. Warships steamed up the Yangtze to Wuhan and battles raged between the two factions of the PLA. Thousands of refugees fled the city. By early August, state media reported that the 'hoodwinked' masses had finally come to their senses.

Showdown in Wuhan

Lin Biao hailed the vanquishing of the Million Heroes as the 'greatest, greatest, greatest' victory, won at the 'tiniest, tiniest cost'. The Central Committee subjected Chen Zaidao to a nine-hour interrogation, during which a member of the Central Cultural Revolution Leading Group slapped him. Zhou Enlai, who was presiding, scolded: 'We are not three-year-olds'.

The triumphant Workers General Headquarters embarked

on a spree of revenge killings. In all, the trouble in Wuhan cost thousands of lives. To prevent similar incidents in the future, the Party leadership demanded a thorough purge of the military, which Lin Biao resisted.

Down With Imperialism!

Marshal Chen Yi had held the post of foreign minister since 1958, but his vocal support for the February Countercurrent saw him forced to step aside, leaving Premier Zhou Enlai back in charge of foreign affairs. At rallies in Beijing, the increasingly radical chants included 'smash all foreign governments'. Zhou Enlai's 'Five Principles of Peaceful Coexistence', the guiding philosophy of the People's Republic of China in its foreign relations from the early 1950s, gave way to calls for 'world revolution'. True believers like Israel Epstein and Sidney Rittenberg helped to manage China's external messaging to the West and the counter-cultural movements of the 1960s created a receptive audience for this new creed.

Reset in foreign relations

Radicals pressured Zhou to recall China's diplomats and transform the missions into propaganda stations for Mao Zedong Thought. Red Guards took over diplomatic posts, even sparking a Red Guard movement among ethnic Chinese in Burma. After the military government there clamped down on the movement, including banning Mao badges, the radicals' violent response led to anti-Chinese rioting. Relations with countries including Nepal, Sri Lanka and Indonesia grew strained.

After Indonesians attacked the Chinese embassy in Jakarta, Red Guards ransacked Indonesia's embassy in Beijing. They also forced their way into the Soviet embassy. After the Mongolian ambassador's chauffeur refused to wear a Mao badge, they set his car on fire. In the northeastern port of Dalian, they beat up the crew of a Soviet ship docked there and paraded its navigator and captain through the streets, also for refusing to wear Mao badges.[41]

David and Nancy Milton were American English teachers at the First Foreign Languages Institute in Beijing from 1964 to 1969. One hot August morning in 1967, they saw students from the institute 'walking down the peaceful, tree-lined road beside the school... carrying cans of gasoline'. With the happy air of summer picnickers, they were on their way, the Miltons later realised, to burn down the British mission.[42]

Of all the former nineteenth-century imperialist powers who had carved out semi-colonial enclaves in Chinese ports and territories, only Great Britain and Portugal retained theirs – Hong Kong and Macao. Local radicals in both places had rioted in sympathy with the Cultural Revolution, attacking colonial era statues and staging strikes. In Macao, a clash with police left eight civilians dead and hundreds wounded. When Red Guards massed at the border, the Portuguese governor apologised for the police's actions.

The stakes were higher in Hong Kong, including for China: the territory's status quo made it a conduit for Chinese international trade and foreign currency earnings. Some manifestations of the Cultural Revolution there verged on the comical, with the Bank of China setting up loudspeakers to blast anti-British propaganda and the British responding with the Beatles. Much of it was deadly serious, however. Maoists in the territory staged strikes and rioted. After Chinese militia and British police skirmished on the border in July, leaving two Chinese and five British dead, both Mao and Zhou tried to placate the radicals there. Not for calming, local Maoists planted over a thousand bombs throughout the territory, killing more than fifty people, including children, and spreading terror. The British responded with strikebreaking measures and mass arrests, including of pro-PRC journalists, while shuttering Communist-affiliated media. Police fired into a violent mob at the governor's mansion, wounding several people. China's official media falsely claimed hundreds had been wounded or killed in a 'bloody massacre', further raising the temperature.

After the Chinese government accused the Beijing-based Reuters journalist Anthony Grey of spying, Red Guards put him under house arrest. They killed his cat and forced him to endure the 'airplane' position until he could see his face reflected in a pool of his own sweat.[43]

The Chinese government demanded the release of eight of the arrested pro-PRC journalists in Hong Kong as a condition for Grey's release. The Hong Kong government relented.

Then the Chinese government demanded the release of thirteen others. Grey would spend 27 months in captivity.

For months, angry crowds had gathered outside the British Mission in Beijing, hurling abuse at the 'imperialists' sheltering inside. On 20 August, the radicals now running the Foreign Ministry gave the British chargé d'affaires Donald Hopson 48 hours to organise the release of two other pro-China journalists and restore the pro-Communist press in Hong Kong.

The radicals also contacted Nie Yuanzi and gave her maps of the mission showing the location of the fuse boxes, water pipes and telephone lines. She ordered her followers to collect screwdrivers and pliers for breaking into the British Mission's store of files. Planning the attack on the building, she ordered anyone who could speak English to be in the vanguard and for everyone to wear dark clothing.

August 1967.
Protests build
outside the
British Mission
in Beijing

On the evening of 22 August 1967, the crowd outside the compound in Beijing had swelled to around 10,000. Aware that the ultimatum would expire at 10:30 p.m., twenty-three diplomats and staff – eighteen men and five women – had gathered in the chancery, which had a strong room for safety. Others, including family members, remained in a separate residential compound. Those in the chancery passed the time eating tinned sausages and peas, drinking claret, playing bridge and watching Peter Sellers in *The Wrong Arm of the Law*.[44]

Hopson had just bid three no-trumps when, at exactly 10:30, a flare went up, horns sounded, and the mob began pouring over the compound's wall, shouting *Sha! Sha! Sha!* (Kill! Kill! Kill!). As they set fire to the mission's vehicles, the British, following an emergency plan codenamed 'Armageddon', retreated to the secure room. But as the building burned, the room filled with smoke. At about 11:10, they pushed open the steel door and fled straight into the hands of a roaring mob. The Red Guards spat on the British, stole their watches, ripped their clothes, beat them with bamboo poles, kicked them and sexually assaulted the women. Female Red Guards grabbed male diplomats by the crotch, these deliberate humiliations recorded by Red Guard photographers. One diplomat could only get a man to stop violently pulling on his wife's ponytail by biting him.

British Mission burns

The People's Liberation Army soldiers assigned to guard the mission eventually came to the rescue of those diplomats who hadn't already escaped to safety. The Party later described the incident as a spontaneous action of 'the outraged masses', though as the diplomat (and future ambassador to China) Percy Cradock reported to the Home Office, it was clearly 'a carefully planned and controlled operation'.

Like more and more things, however, it hadn't been planned or controlled by Mao. The Great Helmsman wasn't pleased. He needed to signal who was boss.

'The Situation is Excellent'

In September 1967, Mao ordered a crackdown on 'ultra-leftists' involved in what was now dubbed the '16 May Conspiracy' against Zhou Enlai. He declared Wang Li and several other members of the Cultural Revolution Leading Group 'bad people'. Mao still hadn't forgiven Wang Li his part in stirring up trouble in Wuhan when he was there. The crackdown would ultimately lead to the arrest of some 3.5 million people.

The politics of the Cultural Revolution are devilishly confusing. They are full of convoluted and improbable conspiracy theories, imagined enemies and absurd proclamations about how brilliantly things were going when they were an absolute mess. Presumed allies such as Mao and his wife Jiang Qing were not always so, while 'frenemies', such as Jiang Qing and

59

Lin Biao, were everywhere. Alliances were constantly, if often subtly, shifting, and contradictory policies and directives rained down from above. At the centre of this unstable world sat Mao, with his paradoxical love of both control and chaos.

By September 1967, only nine out of twenty-nine provinces and regions were run by 'three-way alliance' revolutionary committees. There was still rampant anarchy and killing. Regardless, the following month, Mao declared that 'the situation throughout the country is not just good but excellent and more excellent than it ever has been before'.

In December, the PLA moved to control the organs of public security and justice, an operation that targeted some 34,000 police, 1,100 of whom were killed or driven to suicide. The extent of the army's growing power would be revealed symbolically in a photograph published in January 1968 by the *People's Daily* of Mao, Zhou Enlai and Lin Biao. The order in which leaders appeared in public events and photographs was (and still is) significant and closely observed. In photos of any three leaders, Mao always stood in the centre. In this photo, that place went to Lin Biao.

Lin Biao (briefly) takes centre stage

* * *

In the year since Mao's birthday toast to 'civil war', hundreds of thousands, possibly as many as half a million people had died in violent struggles of one kind or another. Worse was to come.

The Not-So Autonomous Regions

China's policy towards its 'ethnic minority nationalities' had largely been modelled on that of the Soviet Union. The people of the Tibetan, Inner Mongolian, Uyghur and other 'autonomous regions' enjoyed some freedoms regarding religion, language and social customs. Politically, though, they were bound to Party policy and leadership.

As early as 1965, the First Party Secretary of the Inner Mongolian Autonomous Region and PRC Vice-Premier Ulanhu had come under fire for being soft on ethnic Mongolian 'class enemies'. On 6 June 1966, he was arrested and taken to Beijing, accused of opposing Mao and the Cultural Revolution and attempting to make Inner Mongolia independent and capitalist. The Party replaced him with an ethnic Han Chinese.

As was the pattern, anyone associated with Ulanhu became a target as well. The singer Hajab, the son of a humble herding family with an extraordinary gift for *urtiin duu*, an ancient form of Mongolian folk singing, was one. Ulanhu's patronage was enough to get Hajab imprisoned. His jailers tortured him, forcing him to drink their urine to ruin his voice.

Shanghai and Beijing Red Guards swarmed into Inner Mongolia. Together with local radicals, they viciously beat lamas and punished people for speaking Mongolian. Other Mongolians fought them in deadly battles in some rural areas and on the streets of the capital, Hohhot.[45] In early 1967, Red Guards had responded to the call to overthrow local authorities in Inner Mongolia but met ferocious resistance from local workers and regional PLA troops. In April, the 21st Army, loyal to Lin Biao and the central authorities, moved in and declared martial law. By late November, the Inner Mongolian Revolutionary Committee, dominated by Han Chinese and chaired by the commander of the 21st Army, was in charge. A full-scale denunciation campaign began against Ulanhu, now stripped of his posts. Among his many alleged crimes was an imaginary plot by Mongolian women to 'corrupt' Chinese troops.

The pre-revolutionary Inner Mongolian People's Party, or *Nei Ren Dang*, had dissolved in 1947 to merge with the Communist Party. It now stood accused not only of having continued in secret, but of working in cahoots with the Soviet Union and the Soviet-affiliated Mongolian People's Republic as well. An enormous witch-hunt ensued, targeting nearly every Mongol in a position of authority, or with a higher education, or who knew Russian, or who wore the traditional *debel* robe, or was religious – and all their contacts. Round-the-clock interrogations and torture were common. As was typical throughout the Cultural Revolution, the 'investigations' followed the dictum of Beria, Stalin's savage chief of secret police, 'Show me the man and I'll show you the crime'.

From September 1967 to March 1969, more than 2,000 struggle sessions were held in Inner Mongolia. Between 10,000 and 100,000 people lost their lives, a number to suicide, others killed in various ways including being thrown off the top of buildings. Hideous tortures maimed countless others.

Purges in Inner Mongolia

61

Beware Foreign Spies

Jiang Qing made a speech towards the beginning of 1968 warning that some of the foreigners who lived and worked in China were spies. On 18 March, Israel Epstein, who had joined Foreigners targeted the rebels at the Foreign Languages Bureau, was imprisoned on charges of being a 'member of a cabal seeking to dominate China's foreign publicity' and 'an international spy'. Still a believer, during his years in prison he would produce 1,500 pages of earnest, handwritten self-criticism.

On the eve of Labour Day, 1 May, Gladys Yang had gone to bed, leaving her husband Xianyi 'gloomily drinking a bottle of Chinese liquor' in the living room of their apartment. There was a soft knock on the door. A younger colleague asked him to step out into the hallway, which Yang Xianyi did, still wearing his oversized slippers. He soon found himself handcuffed, bundled into a jeep and taken to a crowded prison cell, where the slippers would be his sole footwear for the next four years. One of his cellmates, smelling the *baijiu* on his breath when he arrived, sighed with envy. Yang passed time with his cellmates, who changed from time to time as some were released and others executed, by teaching them songs and poetry he knew by heart, including Ben Jonson's 'Drink to Me Only with Thine Eyes', the Tang epic 'Song of Eternal Regret' and the Scottish song 'Loch Lomond'.

Gladys Yang, arrested not long after, was placed in solitary confinement. She enjoyed better meals and a greater variety of reading matter than her husband, even reading *Das Kapital* for the first time. Solitary confinement nonetheless took a toll on her mental health.

The Cultural Revolution was about to take its most violent turn yet. In late 1967, Chen Boda, the head of the Cultural Revolution Leading Group, alleged that Chiang Kai-shek's KMT, still working to 'recover the mainland' from its base in Taiwan, had Hunting for spies moles working to undermine the Party in Hebei province. Some 84,000 people were investigated for 'treachery' and 3,000 of them were killed. A similar campaign against alleged KMT spies in southwestern Yunnan led to the execution of 14,000 people. These were trial runs for the most vicious and deadly of all the Cultural Revolution campaigns: Cleansing the Class Ranks.

'That's Class Struggle'

In May 1968, the Party declared that members of the Five Black Categories, as well as traitors, spies, capitalist roaders and KMT loyalists, had widely infiltrated the Party and even organisations like the Red Guards. The Campaign to Cleanse the Class Ranks had begun. Even for those times, the campaign was prosecuted in an exceptionally arbitrary and cruel manner, with accusers levelling allegations of conspiracy and disloyalty at people that were impossible to disprove. Across the country, the army led mobs of radicals to attack, torture and kill alleged enemies. Mass murder became commonplace. More than 30 million people became targets, and between 500,000 and 1.5 million were killed. In Shanghai alone, the campaign went after 170,000 people, with 5,500 deaths by torture or suicide.

Campaign to Cleanse the Class Ranks

Southwestern Guangxi was the site of some of the most savage witch-hunts. In at least 400 documented instances mobs not only beat 'class enemies' to death but consumed their flesh, heart and livers in 'cannibal banquets'. In the 1980s, an 86-year-old happily admitted to a researcher that in 1968 he'd killed a teenager and eaten his liver. That's class struggle, he said.[46]

In one county, over just eleven days, local public security officers and militias executed 3,681 class enemies – more than ten times the number of people killed there during the eight years of Japanese invasion and resistance.

The Hundred Day War

One of the most infamous instances of Red Guard-on-Red Guard violence, the 'Hundred Day War' at Beijing's Tsinghua University, broke out in April 1968.

Nie Yuanzi, the lecturer whose big-character poster had inspired 'Bombard the Headquarters', and Kuai Dafu, allies in the past, had become bitter enemies. The conflict between their two groups quickly escalated from mutual recrimination to fistfights to outright battles fought with bows and arrows, catapults, firebombs and home-made tanks. (Tsinghua University boasted an excellent engineering department.) They also employed rockets, grenades and heavy weaponry stolen from the army. Both sides dug tunnels under the campus and dynamited those excavated by the other side.

The fighting spread to other Beijing campuses and spilled into the streets of the capital. Buildings burned. Casualties ran into the hundreds. As the death toll mounted, there were macabre funeral marches to Tiananmen and show trials of captured enemy leaders. Both sides ignored the Party's orders to stop.

Around the hundred-day mark, in late July, the Central Committee mobilised some 30,000 workers from 62 Beijing factories to retake the Tsinghua campus with the help of the Beijing Garrison Command. They called themselves the Capital Workers Mao Zedong Thought Propaganda Team. In the end, more than a hundred thousand people forced their way onto the Tsinghua campus waving Little Red Books and shouting, 'Use arguments, not weapons!'

Nie Yuanzi's faction surrendered and retreated to a neutral part of the campus. Kuai's group attacked the interventionists with stones and spears, killing five and wounding hundreds more. On 27 July, the workers and soldiers laid siege to the buildings where Kuai Dafu and 300 hardcore members of his faction were holed up. It took three days, and more deaths, before the radicals finally gave themselves up.

Kuai Dafu appealed to Mao, who called a meeting with him, Nie and three other Red Guard leaders the following day. Kuai made a theatrical, teary entrance, saying some 'black hand' (backstage manipulator) had sent the workers in to suppress the students. He faced a frosty reception. Mao said that he, Mao, was that 'black hand'. They had all committed 'serious errors'. If they didn't stop fighting, they were no better than Chiang Kai-shek's 'bandits'. He addressed them in a comradely tone, however, and scolded Jiang Qing at one point for speaking down to them.

Kuai's followers decamped to other campuses with most of their weapons - still leaving behind, among other things, 1,435 spears, a variety of guns and rifles, nearly 700 hand grenades, 185 bottles of acid, 25 cannon shells, 50 bottles of poison gas, 168 home-made mines, 16 packs of dynamite and a submachine gun.[47] Searching the buildings on campus, the workers and soldiers discovered weapons-manufacturing workshops, makeshift field hospitals, communications control rooms, torture cells, prisoners and rotting corpses.

Calling for 'restraint, moderation and unity', the Party declared that anyone who kept fighting was a counter-revolutionary and saboteur. As a 26 August *People's Daily* editorial by Yao Wenyuan noted, the 'golden age of the Red Guards' was over. From now on, workers were to 'exercise leadership in everything'.

It was around this time that the painting *Mao Goes to Anyuan* by the Red Guard artist Liu Chunhua appeared. An idealised image of Mao's 1922 journey to Anyuan, Jiangxi province, to help to organise a coal miners' strike, it underscored his bond with China's proletariat. It would become the most iconic artwork of the Cultural Revolution, with some 900 million copies produced. Never mind that it was actually Liu Shaoqi who led the labour movement in Anyuan; a once-celebrated painting of Liu with the Anyuan miners disappeared from sight.

Mangoes – A Sweet Interlude

Mango mania: a gift sent to the workers by a grateful Mao. Many people in northern China had never seen this miraculous fruit before.

On 4 August, on a state visit to Beijing, Pakistani Foreign Minister Mian Arshad Hussain presented Mao with a basket of Sindhri mangoes. The following day, Mao sent the mangoes to the workers' propaganda team that had put an end to the fighting at Tsinghua.

The gift was seen to symbolise Chairman Mao's wisdom, magnanimity and trust in the working class. The workers stayed up all night in their excitement, gazing at and touching the strange and beautiful fruit, which resembled the legendary 'peach of immortality' in traditional iconography.

The mangoes were far too precious to eat. So the workers preserved them in formaldehyde and toured them to factories and colleges for veneration; there were also countless wax replicas in special glass vitrines.

Mango worship spread throughout the country. Mango-themed quilt covers, enamel basins and mugs and mango-flavoured cigarettes were ubiquitous that autumn. The 1 October National Day parade in 1968 featured a float with a giant basket of papier-mâché mangoes. Workers marched behind a banner that read 'The Working Class Must Lead Everything.'

The nation turns Red By then, three-way-alliance revolutionary committees were finally in control everywhere. A rally of 100,000 people in Beijing on 7 September celebrated 'the whole nation turning Red'.

The civil war was over, but the Cultural Revolution was not. The Party permanently expelled from its ranks the imprisoned former president and author of *How To Be A Good Communist*, Liu Shaoqi, declaring him a 'renegade, traitor and scab'. He heard about his expulsion on his seventieth birthday, 24 November, in his prison cell. Due to maltreatment and lack of medical care, he was already suffering from diabetes and high blood pressure, had lost most of his teeth and was just recovering from pneumonia. On hearing the news, his blood pressure shot up. He trembled violently, vomited and never spoke another word.

To the Countryside...

The country's economic situation was deteriorating. The government had to further reduce already meagre cloth and food rations, while more people were needed to help with the harvests. Those living in the overcrowded cities were not, Mao decided, pulling their weight. There appeared to be a solution to all these issues.

Since the 1950s, the Party had encouraged students and white-collar workers to volunteer for work in rural and frontier areas. They could help rural communes with bookkeeping and teach basic literacy while mitigating the problem of urban unemployment. The Socialist Education Movement of 1964 renewed the call for people to *xiàfāng*, or 'go down' to the countryside. It was partly the lukewarm response of so many teachers and school administrators to this idea that had made educators a major target in the early stages of the Cultural Revolution.

In 1968, the Party began to ship public servants, educators and others to rural 'May Seventh Cadre Schools' to do farm work and engage in intensive political study for periods ranging from six months to several years. They would continue to receive their normal salaries. Millions went, though the elderly, the sick and the disabled were exempt.

Among those who had to build their facilities from scratch and prepare virgin land for planting were the staff of the Party's Central Committee. According to the *Peking Review*, these model cadres turned

> ...wasteland into fields and built dormitories and factories on their own. They dug canals, wading knee deep in mud. They went into icy streams to get sand and braved eye-stinging smoke to burn limestone in the kilns. They fought floods to save people's lives and property. They met all these trials head on to gain the revolutionary spirit of 'fearing neither hardship nor death'.

In her memoir *A Cadre School Life: Six Chapters*, Yang Jiang, a writer known for her erudition and gentle wit, presents a more modest picture of life in a cadre school. She describes small joys such as the cups of tea that the rural postal workers would give her husband, a famous intellectual, in exchange for helping them read difficult characters on the envelopes they were sorting. She was chastened to see how the peasants scavenged in the fields for the cabbage stalks and outer leaves that urbanites such as herself discarded as inedible. Farming itself was a humbling experience. Once, bending with great

An unsentimental education

67

anticipation to pull up a carefully-tended root vegetable, she fell on her backside 'tightly clutching a tiny radish with a few spindly roots'.

In late December 1968, Mao ordered all *zhiqing* or 'educated youth' – anyone with at least a junior high school education – to the countryside 'to receive re-education by the poor and lower middle peasantry'. Unlike those sent to May Seventh Cadre Schools, these young people were to be 'sent down' for life.

Exile of the educated youth

In 1969 alone, as many as 2.6 million *zhiqing*, some as young as 14, left the cities for the countryside by train, bus, truck, tractor and on foot. Some began their journey in high spirits, others wept with longing for their families and fear of the unknown. Xi Jinping recalled being the only one in his contingent who was smiling.

Clashes on the Soviet Border

The Soviet invasion of Czechoslovakia in August 1968 alarmed Mao. The *People's Daily* had editorialised at the time that Soviet 'socialist imperialism' was as dangerous as US imperialism. Tensions rose further between the two communist giants. In early March 1969, Chinese and Soviet troops clashed along the Ussuri River, part of the more than 6,400-kilometre border between the two countries. The conflict escalated, with skirmishes occurring far to the west, where Xinjiang bordered the Tajik Soviet Socialist Republic (now Tajikistan).

Sino-Soviet clashes and conciliation

That summer, the Chinese leadership, fearing a nuclear attack, mobilised civilians around the country to dig air raid shelters. It placed the PLA, including its own nascent nuclear forces, on high alert.

After North Vietnamese leader Ho Chi Minh died in September 1969, both Zhou Enlai and the Soviet Premier Alexei Kosygin went to Hanoi to pay their respects. Although they timed their attendance to avoid meeting up, the North Vietnamese were keen to broker a truce between their two biggest allies. The last time Kosygin had tried to speak to the Chinese leadership, the operator in Zhongnanhai had called him a 're-visionist' and hung up. Now, on the urging of the Vietnamese, he flew to Beijing for a tense four-hour discussion with Zhou Enlai during which they agreed to withdraw their forces to a specified distance from the border. The talks took place in the Beijing airport because Zhou refused Kosygin entry into the city itself.

'A Great Victory'

On 1 April 1969, one month after the outbreak of the border war, the Party convened its Ninth Party Congress. Although Party congresses were supposed to occur every five years, it had been over a decade since the last one. There were fewer officials, more members of the army and many newcomers among the record 1,512 delegates, a mix reflected in the new khaki-heavy Central Committee as well.

The congress heralded the 'great victory' of the Cultural Revolution, reinstated the Party's ruling Politburo and dissolved the Cultural Revolution Leading Group, whose remaining five members, including Jiang Qing, were given places in the Politburo. The congress affirmed that 'Comrade Lin Biao is Comrade Mao Zedong's close comrade-in-arms and successor.'

Declaration of victory

Mao ordered all fighting to cease and Red Guard organisations to disband. Industrial and agricultural production began to recover. On 12 June 1969, on Mao's instructions, the Party banned the further manufacture of Mao badges and ceramic busts and told people to refrain from performing the Loyalty Dance or bowing to his portrait. The worship, in his view, had become excessive.

Also winding up in late 1969 was the exceptionally savage campaign against the non-existent Inner Mongolian People's Party. The Communist Party nonetheless carved out parts of Inner Mongolia and placed them under the jurisdiction of five bordering provinces to forestall any moves towards ethnic separatism, shrinking the autonomous region's total territory from 1.2 million square kilometres in 1966 to 0.4 million.

Death of Liu Shaoqi

Liu Shaoqi died just over a year after his expulsion from the Party, on 12 November 1969. In great secrecy but with little respect, military guards transported his body, wrapped in a sheet with his feet protruding, to a crematorium.

PART FOUR

1970–76: The Ups and Downs of Winding Down

Everyone will die, but death varies in significance.

Mao Zedong

In January 1970, Mao launched a new campaign, called 'One Strike and Three Antis' (strike against counter-revolutionaries; anti-graft, anti-profiteering and anti-waste). It was meant to address the mounting economic crisis. But the vagueness of its targets, and the ease with which a person could be labelled a 'counter-revolutionary' in a time of mob justice, resulted in further wanton violence. Over the next two years, this campaign would cost some 200,000 people their lives (including the young anti-Bloodline Theory activist Yu Luoke).

About one in eight Chinese people became a direct target of the Cleansing of the Class Ranks or the One-Strike, Three Antis campaign, or were closely related to someone who was.[48] A third major campaign, this one aimed at an alleged '16 May Counter-Revolutionary Clique', ran from February 1971 to the end of the Cultural Revolution in 1976 and claimed another estimated 100,000 lives.

The Third Kind of People
The People's Republic had not had a head of state, or 'president' (*guójiā zhǔxí*), since Liu Shaoqi was purged. In 1970, Mao proposed amending the Chinese constitution to abolish the office altogether (and, implicitly, any pretence to a Party/state balance of power).

Lin Biao and the radical theorist Chen Boda vociferously disagreed: there should be a president – and Mao should be it. Mao, who had no interest in the ceremonial duties of the presidency, reportedly quoted the third century statesman-general

Cao Cao who, when urged to declare himself emperor, said people might as well throw him straight onto the fire to cook. Zhou Enlai, ever sensitive to which way the wind was blowing, switched from supporting the idea of a presidency to opposing it.

Lin Biao was also now pushing his 'theory of genius', a kind of 'great man' theory of history. Mao, whose Thought he'd described as a 'spiritual atom bomb of infinite power', was the 'genius' in question. Mao suspected that Lin Biao wanted the presidency retained so he could one day occupy it, and that the 'theory of genius' was intended to lay the groundwork for a similar cult around himself and his 'super genius' son Lin Liguo. Lin Biao had been smoothing the way for his son's future ascension, having promoted the 25-year-old well beyond his talents to deputy director of the Air Force General Office and deputy director of the Combat Division of the PLA.

Lin Biao oversteps the mark

Mao always said that power came from the barrel of a gun, but it had to be the Party who commanded the gun. Under Lin Biao, the army had not always obeyed the Party. What's more, during the border crisis with the Soviet Union, Lin Biao had issued major commands without the Party's authorisation, including for the evacuation of whole cities. When Mao was shown that order in writing he was so angry he burnt it.[49]

These tensions came to a head at a Party plenum in Lushan in the summer of 1959. Lushan was the same mountain retreat where the previous army chief, Peng Dehuai, had infuriated Mao in 1958 by criticising the Great Leap Forward. Now Mao accused Lin Biao and Chen Boda of committing serious 'political errors'.

The conflict between Mao and Lin Biao was increasingly apparent to the rest of the leadership, even if it was hidden from the public. Mao hinted at it in a rambling five-hour conversation towards the end of 1970 with Edgar Snow. Mao admitted to Snow that the violence of the Cultural Revolution had been excessive. He also said that he was sick of always being referred to as 'Great Leader, Great Commander, Great Helmsman and Great Teacher'. He remarked that he liked 'reactionaries' like the famously anti-communist US President Richard Nixon, because at least they were honest. By contrast, in his world there were 'three kinds of people': sincere admirers, 'those who drift with the tide', and 'the people who pretend to admire you'. The last type, he said, couldn't be trusted.

Snow concluded his report for *Life Magazine* with an anecdote: 'As he courteously escorted me to the door, he said he was not a complicated man, but really very simple. He was, he said, only a lone monk walking the world with a leaky umbrella'. Snow had not only missed the jibes against Lin Biao, who had authored the Great-this-Great-that formulation that so irked Mao, but he'd also misunderstood the Chinese pun about the monk. A monk with an umbrella is a person with no hair and no sky, *wúfǎ wútiān* – a homonym for 'utterly lawless'. Mao was saying he was above the law.

A monk with an umbrella

* * *

One day in September 1971, Israel Epstein was sitting out his third year in solitary confinement in Qincheng Prison when the guards burst into his cell and, without explanation, snatched away his Little Red Book and other reading matter. When they returned the book, it was missing Lin Biao's preface. Nien Cheng, in Shanghai's No. 1 Detention Centre, had a similar experience and was thunderstruck by the possibility that Lin Biao could be in disgrace.

Around the country, the top commanders of China's ten major military regions were put on high alert but not told why. Military and civilian flights were briefly grounded as well. When the grand celebrations for National Day on 1 October were cancelled, everyone knew something big had happened, but few knew exactly what. Then they realised that Lin Biao was absent from the kind of public events he'd typically attended as defence minister and second in command. The news began to leak – Lin Biao, the traitor, was dead.

* * *

A few months earlier, Lin Biao had retired to his summer villa at the leadership's coastal resort at Beidaihe, upset and in ill health. His wife Ye Qun and son Lin Liguo joined him. They passed the days watching films, including *Patton*, and listened to talks on Alexander the Great. On 7 September, Ye Qun received a delivery of some Russian–Chinese dictionaries and Russian conversation primers. On the evening of 12

Disappearance of Lin Biao

September, the trio suddenly sped off in Lin Biao's bulletproof Red Flag limousine towards a nearby airport. There, together with several close aides and a pilot, they boarded a Hawker Siddeley Trident jet. Without waiting for the co-pilot, navigator or radio operator, or even for the jet to finish refuelling, they took off, in such a rush that they clipped a truck on the runway, damaging a wing light.

Lin Liguo's sister alerted the leadership, reportedly accusing her mother and brother of kidnapping her beloved father and forcing him to flee. Zhou Enlai wanted to shoot the plane down, to which Mao responded, 'Rain will fall. Widows will remarry. Let him go.' In the early hours of 13 September, not long after taking off, the plane crashed and burned in Outer Mongolia, killing all on board.

Wreckage of Lin Biao's plane in the Gobi Desert in Mongolia, 13 Sept. 1971

The Party broke the news that Lin Biao was dead to officials in late October and to the public in November. It would be another seven months – and many rumours and partial revelations later – before it released its official report. The gist was that security forces learned that Lin was plotting to assassinate Mao and carry out a coup d'état. After Lin realised he'd been found out, he tried to flee to the Soviet Union. Unsurprisingly, a plethora of sensational details and alternative explanations emerged, including rumours that Lin Liguo had been the plotter-in-chief. The truth may never be known.

The incident affected Mao deeply. His health had been poor

for some time, but after Lin Biao's death he had more trouble sleeping than usual, suffered swelling in his legs and feet and began slurring his words. Within a year he would suffer non-fatal congestive heart failure.

The shock for regular citizens was huge as well. The years of relentless violence and destruction had already left many disillusioned, confused and grieving. Now they wondered: if Lin Biao had been so monstrously bad, why had Mao placed so much faith in him? Was Mao's judgement that poor?

Old certainties overturned

The PLA's prestige and power plummeted. Those who had supported Lin Biao suddenly found themselves on the wrong side. Wang Shuhua, the radical Ming Tombs tour guide who had led the assault on the emperor Wanli's remains, lost her job. Conversely, Chen Zaidao, whose Million Heroes organisation had been attacked on Lin Biao's orders, was back in favour.

* * *

Fu Ning, the adopted daughter of Politburo member Ye Jianying, was a young rocket scientist doing a stint at a May Seventh Cadre School when the news about Lin Biao filtered through. At the start of the Cultural Revolution she'd been so ardent a supporter that, she wrote, she wished it were possible for young people to 'give up a year of their life so that Chairman Mao could live one minute longer'.[50] But now she stood accused of membership in the spurious '16 May Conspiracy' and was nervously waiting to be sent to prison. After Lin Biao died, her problem evaporated. This led her to consider how elite power struggles impacted the lives of innocent people in non-democratic societies like her own. These insights would inspire her future career as an independent investigative journalist and historian, writing under the pen name of Dai Qing, just as the senseless environmental destruction she'd witnessed at the cadre school would lead her to become one of China's first environmental activists.

The Enemy of My Enemy is My Friend

In the absence of diplomatic relations, when the Chinese and American leadership needed to communicate they passed on messages via third parties including Pakistani and Romanian diplomats. Despite Cold War hostility, by the start of the

1970s both sides were concerned enough about the impact of the deepening Vietnam War on regional stability, as well as the nuclear and other ambitions of the Soviet Union, to want to forge a connection.

The death of Lin Biao, who had opposed rapprochement with the United States, seemed to have cleared a major obstacle on the Chinese side. President Nixon, meanwhile, was impressed by a positive report on Mao's China in the *Atlantic Monthly* by the academic Ross Terrill. His national security adviser, Henry Kissinger, had no problem dealing with dictatorships so long as it served US interests.

Ping Pong diplomacy

Few Americans apart from the safely sympathetic Snow and some Black Panthers had ever been permitted to visit the PRC. In April 1971, the US table tennis team was competing at the World Table Tennis Championships in Nagoya, Japan alongside the Chinese team. An unplanned but friendly exchange on a bus between a Chinese and American player made the news. Several other countries' teams planned to visit China after the tournament. China extended the invitation to the Americans.

On his return from China, one of the American players marvelled:

> People are just like us. They are real, they're genuine, they got feeling... The country is similar to America, but still very different. It's beautiful. They got the Great Wall, they got plains over there. They got an ancient palace, the parks, there's streams, and they got ghosts that haunt; there's all kinds of, you know, animals. The country changes from the south to the north. The people, they have... a unity. They really believe in their Maoism.[51]

'Ping Pong diplomacy' was the first sign of warming Sino-American relations. Australia, Japan and two dozen other countries had also begun the process of normalising relations with China. Zhou apologised to the British for the sacking and burning of the mission and said China would pay for its reconstruction.

Chinese table tennis player Zhuang Zedong (left) presents a silk print to his US counterpart Glenn Cowan at the 1971 World Championships in Nagoya, Japan.

In October 1971, the United Nations gave the China seat in the UN to the People's Republic, expelling Chiang Kai-shek's government in Taiwan. Beijing immediately insisted that the UN recognise that Hong Kong and Macao were not colonial possessions but occupied Chinese sovereign territory. By agreeing, the General Assembly denied the people of Hong Kong and Macao any legal claim to self-determination thereafter.

The people of China learned of Nixon's impending visit in late October 1971. The guards at the prison where Nien Cheng was held ordered the prisoners to listen to a special broadcast. Praising the 'excellent situation created by the Great Proletarian Cultural Revolution', the presenter explained that Nixon's request to visit China signalled the decay of capitalism and an acknowledgement by Washington that its previous China policy had been a mistake. This was not a backflip on the part of the Chinese leadership but 'a great victory'.

On 21 February 1972, US Air Force One touched down in Beijing. The eight-day trip was the first visit of an American president to the People's Republic and the first sign of a thaw in two decades of Cold War. On the tarmac to greet President Richard Nixon and First Lady Pat Nixon was a smiling Zhou Enlai. Zhou waited for Nixon to extend his hand before reaching out to shake it. Zhou's hypervigilant attention to symbolism and detail was a key to his success both as a diplomat and political survivor.

Mao, despite a serious recent health scare, insisted on meeting Nixon soon after his arrival. Echoing his words to Snow, he reassured the president that he was relatively happy to see right-wing people in power.

Nixon and Mao shake hands in 1972.

Zhou Enlai accompanied the Nixons to a children's hospital in Beijing, an acrobatics display in Shanghai, a boat tour of Hangzhou's scenic West Lake and of course the Great Wall. Treated to a performance of the revolutionary model ballet *Red Detachment of Women*, the Nixons asked Jiang Qing who had written and directed the spectacular. She bemused them with her answer: 'the masses.' On the last day in Beijing, they toured the Forbidden City, as blissfully unaware of the frantic restoration that preceded their visit as they were of the intensity and violence of the campaigns still scything through the population.

On the last day of the visit, 27 February, Nixon and Zhou Enlai signed the Shanghai Communique that Kissinger had previously helped to draft and was part of the precondition for the visit. The English version stated that the US 'acknowledged' that 'all Chinese on either side of the Taiwan Strait maintain there is but one China'. The Chinese version used a stronger word, *chéngrèn*, which implied agreement and acceptance.

Even the English was too much for the conservative American commentator William F Buckley Jr, who accompanied the Nixons on the trip and declared that it signalled the loss of 'any remaining sense of moral mission in the world'.

The visit, which Nixon called 'the week that changed the world', achieved a mutual objective – each country neutralised the threat that the other might align with their mutual enemy, the Soviet Union. It also served Beijing's goal of driving a wedge between Taiwan and its most important ally and opened fresh paths to foreign trade and investment. It was a triumph for Zhou, who appeared to cement his position as successor to a visibly ailing Mao. Jiang Qing and the radicals seethed, waiting for him to make a mistake they could capitalise on.

Domestic Conciliations

On 6 January 1972, one month before Nixon's visit, Chen Yi, the foreign minister side-lined during the Red Guard takeover of the foreign ministry, passed away from cancer at the age of 70. His funeral took place at the national cemetery of Babaoshan on a freezing afternoon four days later. Mao had not planned to attend. At the last minute, he changed his mind, threw a greatcoat over his pyjamas and headed for the cemetery.

Among the other mourners was the Cambodian Prince Norodom Sihanouk. Mao told Sihanouk that he now understood that Chen Yi's opposition to the radical line embraced by Lin Biao and others had been a principled one.

Following the funeral, the Party 'rehabilitated' a number of people, recalling them from internal exile, releasing them from detention and allowing them to go back to work. Gladys Yang and her husband were quietly freed. Yang Xianyi, released first, returned to a dusty apartment with rat-gnawed carpets, piled up furniture – and the half-drunk bottle of *baijiu* right where he'd left it. Others who would be released over the following two years included Israel Epstein and Nien Cheng, as well as Luo Ruiqing, the PLA chief of staff who'd tried to commit suicide in 1966 and lost a leg as a result. The first thing Luo did, confounding his daughter, was to go to Tiananmen and salute Mao's portrait.

First
'rehabilitations'

Zhou Enlai was diagnosed with gallbladder cancer in May 1972. Mao, for obscure reasons, ordered the doctors to keep Zhou in the dark about his true condition and secretly refused his second in command the lifesaving operation he needed. Zhou, visibly unwell, continued to work at a punishing pace, including on a new campaign to criticise Lin Biao's 'anti-Party clique'. He still had the energy to take a dig at Jiang Qing's cultural politics, including her insistence that 'the masses' were the authors of everything. The premier chided a PLA cultural troupe in Guangzhou whose performance he saw in April that year for not announcing the names of their soloists and accompanists, saying their 'extreme leftist way of thinking' made it impossible to 'raise artistic standards'.

The Party encouraged people to produce amateur ('worker and peasant') performances using traditional regional costumes, songs and dances and even local dialects and languages. This was not an invitation to stray beyond political bounds, however. One officially lauded show from Xinjiang bore the scintillating title 'Implement Total Dictatorship over the Bourgeoisie'. Jiang Qing was vexed by the directions some of this unfettered creativity was taking: 'They're wearing red stars and waving red flags, but they're swing dancing,' she complained. 'They may as well be naked.'[52]

Song and dance in the approved manner

In 1970, some universities had recruited new classes of students for the first time since 1966. Only workers, peasants and soldiers could apply, and only after completing two years at a farm or factory, and then only on the recommendation of Party cadres. The last was a pathway to corruption, with cadres infamously ushering in connections through the back door.

In 1972, an ailing Zhou Enlai, keen to advance Chinese science and technology, exempted students studying social and natural sciences from the requirement to engage in manual labour for two years before starting university. Although there was still no national entrance examination, some universities began holding their own exams, with State Council approval.

A radical 23-year-old 'educated youth' named Zhang Tiesheng derailed the examination system almost as soon as it had begun. Zhang handed in a blank (or nearly so) exam paper, on the back of which he wrote indignantly that he'd only had two days to prepare because he'd been working in the fields eighteen hours a day, preoccupied with harvests and self-struggle. Otherwise, he would have aced it. There was no point competing with 'bookworms who have never done a day of honest work', who 'disgusted' him. Jiang Qing and others declared him a hero, exams were annulled and countless bookworms who'd laboured by day and studied by night for the exams plunged into despair.

It was a political setback for Zhou, and not the only one that year. Encouraged by the success of Nixon's visit, he had invited the left-wing Italian filmmaker Michelangelo Antonioni to shoot a documentary in China, giving him a relatively free pass to go where he liked. No Westerner had ever been given such an opportunity. The resulting film, *Chung Kuo*, was released in late 1972. It featured unfiltered observations of ordinary life, from food prep to a black-market transaction. It couldn't have been more different from China's own heroic self-presentation. Chinese officials tried, with mixed success, to stop it from screening in Europe. The Party launched a massive campaign, complete with children's songs, to denounce Antonioni for deliberately trying to 'humiliate' China. It didn't matter that none of the film's hyperventilating critics had even seen the film. For a gratified Jiang Qing and her fellow radicals, it provided yet another cudgel with which to beat Zhou.

A fresh scandal for Zhou Enlai

Antonioni himself was shocked by the reaction, especially since Chinese diplomats in Rome had been among the first to view it and had thanked him for his 'affectionate' view of their country. *Chung Kuo* screened publicly in China for the first time in 2004, to acclaim.

Mao also gave the radicals reason to gnash their teeth when, in 1973, he summoned Deng Xiaoping back to Beijing from the tractor factory in Jiangxi province where he had been sent to labour. Deng agreed with Zhou that China badly needed the 'Four Modernisations' of agriculture, industry, defence and science and technology. He threw himself into exploring possibilities for political and economic reform.

Nixon's visit had sparked interest from American consumers in China and Chinese goods. Stylish New Yorkers snapped up 'Chairman Mao jackets' imported by Dragon

Lady Traders while the teen magazine *Ingenue* advised young Americans how to capture the 'essence of Chinese beauty' with smooth round bobs and eye makeup for 'almost oval eyes'.[53] In 1974, the annual Canton Trade Fair, where foreign businesses went to make deals, moved to a new, bigger venue decorated with red balloons and dangling streamers bearing quotations from Mao.

Increased trade, especially the export of Chinese oil and textiles, gave Beijing's coffers a much-needed boost, which was fortunate because drought had also impelled China to import record amounts of US wheat, cotton, soybeans and corn. Mao was beginning to put the pursuit of development for the 'Third World' at the centre of China's foreign policy rather than world revolution. In early 1973, he approved a proposal by Zhou Enlai to spend $4.3 billion (approximately the total annual value of China's foreign trade at the time) on importing heavy industrial equipment from the West. China needed more industrial capacity; the West had too much. It was win-win for all except the radicals. They strenuously opposed both commerce with capitalist countries and the de-linking of industrial production from the military, seeing in it the end of revolutionary China's spirit of self-sufficiency. Towards the end of 1973, they subjected Zhou to prolonged and intense criticism in high-level meetings, even calling him a 'traitor'. Mao let this go on for a while before eventually bringing the episode to an end with a warm public handshake.

Down to the Country

Some 'sent-down' youth were lucky not to have to go too far from home. Others were exiled to remote and unforgiving environments like the Great Northeast Wilderness, with its brutal winters, or the tropical jungles of Yunnan in the southwest, where they laboured on such projects as levelling old growth forests for rubber plantations. State-run farms, fisheries and plantations generally offered better conditions than collectively owned farms.

Villagers were ambivalent about these newcomers, who came with soft hands that had never laboured and hungry teenage mouths, though welcoming the tools, soap and

82

candles they brought with them from the city as well as their contributions as 'barefoot doctors' and teachers. The poverty, deprivation and backwardness in the villages, where electrification was rare and running water non-existent in most cases, shocked the young people – it was so different from the happy, prosperous countryside of propaganda.

Despite the hardship, some sent-down youth also found freedom, including the freedom to think about and discuss the violence they'd perpetrated, witnessed or been subject to. Had they been used as pawns in a larger political struggle? Lied to? Betrayed? Many read voraciously in search of answers. The early twentieth-century writer Lu Xun's acerbic commentary on the politics and society of his time acquired fresh resonance, as did classics such as *The Records of the Grand Historian Sima Qian*, with its sharp observations on tyranny. Russian novels including Ethel Lilian Voynich's *The Gadfly* were highly sought-after, as were translations produced with yellow or grey covers for 'internal reference', including works by Sartre and Kerouac and *Waiting for Godot*.

Freedom in isolation

Poetry was enormously popular, from the ancient *Book of Songs* to translations of foreign poets including T.S. Eliot, Whitman, Mayakovsky and Neruda that inspired a new poetic idiom in Chinese.[54] Poetry, more than fiction, was easy to read, write, memorise, pass around – and hide.

A young poet, Guo Lusheng (penname Shizhi), became an icon among sent-down youth. Guo had been a member of an informal poetry collective that came under attack early in the Cultural Revolution. As other members of the group were murdered or committed suicide, Guo suffered a mental breakdown but continued to write. His poems, passed on by hand or mouth, electrified his peers and helped inspire an underground poetry movement that would burst into the open after Mao's death. His 'Believe in the Future' expressed the anguish, defiance and hope of his generation.

> *When my purple grapes have turned into deep autumn dew*
> *When my fresh flowers lie in another's embrace*
> *I will stubbornly use the frozen withered vine*
> *To write on the desolate land: Believe in the future.*

The Ongoing Problem of Lin Biao

A debate about how to frame Lin Biao's betrayal laid bare the split in the Party between the radical faction around Jiang Qing and Zhou Enlai and other relative 'moderates'. According to Zhou, Lin Biao had been guilty of 'ultraleftism'. According to Jiang Qing, he had been an 'ultrarightist'. Words had lost their meaning but not their political significance. In the end, Mao pronounced Lin Biao an 'ultrarightist and revisionist'. His 'leftism' had been fake. He had 'waved the Red Flag to defeat the Red Flag'. It was still right to be left.

Having it both ways

The Tenth Party Congress that convened in August 1973 reflected the lack of a coherent line. Recent purges had left the Party's Central Committee severely depleted. The relatively moderate Deng Xiaoping and the Mongolian leader Ulanhu were now welcomed back into the fold. At the same time, the radicals rose within the Party hierarchy, with Jiang Qing gaining a seat in the Politburo and her associate Zhang Chunqiao promoted to the all-powerful Politburo Standing Committee. By playing off opposing factions, Mao, as usual, was having it both ways.

Following the congress, a new campaign to 'Criticise Lin Biao and Confucius' was born. Confucianism valued moderation, learning and people knowing their place. But it hadn't been a major influence on politics or been in intellectual fashion since the early twentieth century. Red Guards had already trashed the sage's ancestral home. This seemingly curious turn of events was partly to do with Mao's obsession with the anti-Confucian philosophy of Legalism. The ancient tyrant Qin Shihuang (259–210 BCE), to whom Mao liked to compare himself, had also been a fan. The new campaign demanded that people rekindle their ire at Confucius for having been a feudal, hierarchy-entrenching, women-oppressing slave owner. Jiang Qing focused on Confucius's views on women as a way of promoting gender equality, but Mao read this as a play for more power and, annoyed, cut off her access to him.

At a meeting with Kissinger held around this time, Mao jokingly offered the American 'tens of thousands of Chinese women', saying, 'You know China is a very poor country. We don't have much. What we have in excess is women.'

After Kissinger quipped there were no quotas or tariffs for women, Zhou nervously added that it would have to be on 'a voluntary basis'.

To publicly associate Lin Biao – doyen of armed struggle and advocate of egalitarianism in the ranks – with Confucius, who preached social harmony and a strict social hierarchy in which soldiers occupied the lowest rung, had always been a stretch. In a not-so-subtle barb at the premier, Jiang Qing and her coterie pointed the campaign instead at a more logical target: Confucius's historical idol, the Duke of Zhou.

Among the campaign's 'model' activists were a group of saleswomen in the household goods section of the Beijing Friendship Store (mainly serving foreign residents and visitors). They had devoted a year and a half to studying 'Lin Biao's deviations' until 'they were able to distinguish between bourgeois apriorism and genuine dialectical materialism'. They also 'launched an offensive against male chauvinism' at the store on International Women's Day.[55] So far as the majority of Chinese people were concerned, however, it was one campaign too many. Most simply went through the motions.

Cultural Revolution fatigue

There were still plenty of these motions to go through, as politics relentlessly intruded on every aspect of life. The Australian sinologist Geremie Barmé, who was studying at Liaoning University, recalled how loudspeakers woke the students every day at 6:00 a.m., haranguing them to 'Enhance physical education, improve the People's strength, be on high alert and defend the motherland!' It was the start of the day's blistering soundtrack of revolutionary updates, 'punctuated with martial music and rousing exhortations'.

* * *

Around this time, the Portuguese dictatorship fell. The new government in Lisbon offered to hand Macao back to Beijing, but the Party had enough on its plate and declined. Mao's time was running out. At the Tenth Party Congress his doctors had to install an oxygen tank at the podium where he'd be speaking. He would soon be diagnosed with fatal amyotrophic lateral sclerosis, otherwise known as Lou Gehrig's disease. Anyone wanting to see him had to go through his carer Zhang Yufeng, a former attendant on his special train.

Rumblings of Discontent

Lin Biao's posthumous reversal of fortune led many of the traumatised survivors of campaigns he'd supported to demand justice. Some women widowed by the violence revived an ancient form of protest – loud, public lament. Laying siege to the homes of officials, they wailed piteously for attention. Other victims besieged the homes and offices of those who had persecuted them. The detested chairman of Nanjing University's Revolutionary Committee scarcely dared to leave his home. Eventually he had to be transferred to another province to avoid his accusers.[56]

Abuse of privilege

In January, the confessions of the son of a high-level military official who admitted he'd only got into Nanjing University because of his father's connections, sparked more protests against the abuse of special privileges by Party and state cadres. While the Party sanctioned the grassroots campaign against 'cadres going through the back door', the generals and other leaders objected when it began to hit closer to home.

The countryside wasn't free from corruption, either. With sent-down youth clamouring for permission to return home, many local officials squeezed the men for cigarettes and liquor and harassed the women for sex. In April 1974, ten thousand sent-down youth demonstrated in Nanjing, demanding their urban residence permits back. They held a sit in, blocked the trains and built a shantytown. The central leadership told the local authorities to accede to the protesters' demands and calm down the situation. But the rustication policy remained in place. Elsewhere, young people who'd made it back to the cities clashed violently with authorities trying to force them back to the countryside. Within a year, some two million sent-down youth would make it back to the cities one way or another. Many who had settled and married peasants were filled with regret, now trapped in a destiny they'd assumed was set in stone.

Writing under the collective name 'Li Yi Zhe', three young men from Guangzhou (the former Red Guards **Li** Zhengtian, Chen **Yi**yang and Wang Xi**zhe**) wrote a lengthy and incendiary big-character poster titled 'On Socialist Democracy and the Chinese Legal System'. Denouncing the trend towards 'social-fascist dictatorship', it appealed for 'socialist democracy and law', saying the essential conflict in China was between a powerful, privileged and manipulative Party elite and the powerless masses. While focussing their criticism on Lin Biao, it was clearly aimed at Jiang Qing and her fellow radicals as well. The authors sent the essay to the Party Centre in Beijing as well as provincial authorities.

Although the trio was arrested, their essay, copied and widely distributed in *samizdat* form, excited widespread if whispered debate. The big-character poster had broken out of its cage. It was no longer just a tool of radical Maoist politics. Other *dàzìbào* appeared that blamed Jiang Qing and her radical clique for a declining social order, struggling economy and cultural and educational decay. In some cases, local authorities tacitly or even openly supported these dissident voices.

On Mao's 81st birthday, the Chairman summoned Zhou to his quarters for a talk just after midnight. The Cultural Revolution would soon end, he said, but there'd no doubt be a new one every seven or eight years for a long time to come.

In January 1975, the Party enshrined in the constitution the 'Four Great Freedoms' – to 'speak freely', to 'openly air views', to carry out 'big debates' and to post big-character posters. It was not a good idea to take this too literally.

The Four Great Freedoms

Zhang Zhixin was nineteen when the People's Republic was founded in 1949. She joined the Party six years later and worked as a cadre in a provincial propaganda department. During the three-year famine, she grew critical of Mao's leadership. She continued to voice her strong opinions despite the fevered atmosphere of the Cultural Revolution, excoriating Jiang Qing for destroying Chinese culture and even defending Liu Shaoqi and others under attack.

In 1968, Zhang was sent to a May Seventh Cadre School, but refused to repent: 'It is better to live with honesty than flattery.' Handed a commuted death sentence in 1969, she remained defiant in prison, where she endured horrific forms of torture, including confinement in a cell too cramped to stand up in and frequent sexual assault by guards and fellow prisoners, who were rewarded with shorter sentences. She rubbed her own faeces into her skin in a desperate attempt to stop the abuse.

In late 1973, the leadership decided, after much debate, that she could be useful in the ongoing campaign to criticise Lin Biao and brought her onstage at a rally. She denounced Mao and Jiang Qing instead. Two years later, she was executed; the guards slit her vocal cords first so she couldn't shout her defiance.

* * *

The mass killings that began in September 1966 had still not ended. In late July 1975, the military assaulted several villages and the town of Shadian in southwestern Yunnan province, places with a mostly ethnic Muslim Hui population. Early on in the Cultural Revolution, Red Guards had destroyed mosques and burned Korans there. In 1974, villagers travelled to the provincial capital of Kunming to demand their freedom to worship but were turned away for 'causing a disturbance'. The following year they tried to re-open the mosques. With Mao's approval, Deng Xiaoping, then PLA Chief of Staff, ordered in the army, which razed the town and murdered some 1,600 unarmed residents, including children, the elderly and infirm.[57]

In 1975, Mao reiterated calls for 'unity'. He proclaimed the success of the Cultural Revolution – speaking of it, as he had in 1969, as something that was finished. In May, he chastised Jiang Qing, Zhang Chunqiao, Yao Wenyuan and Wang Hongwen for ignoring the Politburo, pretending to act on his authority and – introducing the phrase – acting like a 'Gang of Four'.

Neither did Mao fully trust Deng or Zhou, who wanted to free science from the constraints of ideology to better serve the cause of modernisation. He worried that they would negate the Cultural Revolution and his legacy altogether. But in early 1976, before he could have Deng purged a second time, Zhou Enlai died. His death shook the nation.

The Death of Zhou Enlai and the Tiananmen Incident
On 11 January, in the freezing pre-dawn hours, hundreds of thousands of people lined Beijing's east-west Chang'an Avenue. When finally, late that afternoon, a black-and-white hearse at the centre of a motorcade passed on its way westward to the cemetery at Babaoshan, they began to weep.

Historians still debate Zhou's legacy and role in the Cultural Revolution. Was he a moderating force, or Mao's great enabler? The Harvard scholar Roderick MacFarquhar likened him to 'a superb horseman attempting to stay on and ultimately control a bolting horse'. The sinologist Pierre Ryckmans (pen name Simon Leys) called him 'the staunchest pillar of a regime that managed to kill more innocent Chinese citizens in twenty-five years of peace than had the combined forces of all foreign imperialists in one hundred years of endemic aggression'. In the (largely persistent) popular view of the time in China, however, he was something of a hero who had been both willing and able to mitigate some of the horror of the previous decade.

Zhou Enlai's mixed legacy

Mao did not attend Zhou's modest state memorial, at which Deng Xiaoping delivered the eulogy. Days later, Deng was relieved of his duties as senior vice-premier and the minister of public security, Hua Guofeng, was named the new premier. After that Deng attended Politburo meetings grudgingly. He feigned deafness when attacked by the likes of Zhang Chunqiao, who'd coveted the position of premier himself and was also in a foul mood.

Jiang Qing and her allies banned further public mourning of Zhou, including the wearing of black armbands and the placing of wreaths. After the Shanghai *Wenhui Daily*, a newspaper aligned with the radical faction, appeared to call Zhou 'the biggest capitalist-roader in the Party', angry Shanghainese surrounded its offices in protest. They plastered trains leaving Shanghai with big-character posters denouncing the newspaper, helping to spread the ferment well beyond the city.

Across the country, protests mounted. On 4 April, the eve of the Qingming festival to honour the dead, tens of thousands of people poured into Tiananmen Square in Beijing defiantly bearing wreaths, banners and posters. Their speeches and poems obliquely criticised Mao ('Gone for good is Qin Shihuang's feudal society') and overtly vented anger at 'the White-Boned demon', the evil ghoul from *Journey to the West* that now clearly stood in for Jiang Qing:

In my grief I hear demons shriek.
I weep while wolves and jackals laugh.

Though tears I shed to mourn a hero,
With head raised high, I draw my sword.[58]

There had been many collective actions and rebellions over the past ten years. This was the first one directed at the Cultural Revolution itself.

With Mao's blessing, militias aligned with the Gang of Four pushed onto the square and ripped down posters and removed wreaths, skirmishing with protesters. A police command post burned. It took the arrival of some ten thousand security forces to disperse the crowd with beatings and arrests. Similar scenes around the country are believed to have resulted in thousands of deaths.

The Party condemned the 'Tiananmen Incident' as counter-revolutionary, purging Deng Xiaoping for a second time as an alleged instigator of the trouble. The 'Gang of Four' wanted Deng to be dragged out in public to be struggled by the masses, but Wang Dongxing, Mao's head of security, smuggled Deng and his family to a safehouse before they could act.

Not long afterwards, Xinhua News Agency revealed that in early March a meteor shower had fallen over northeastern Jilin province. A sudden thunderous noise had terrified people, who feared they were under nuclear attack by the Soviet Union. Then a giant red fireball larger than a full moon had shot across the sky, before exploding and scattering a total of four tonnes of fragments over an area of 500 square kilometres.

Signs and portents

In traditional times, such cosmic events signalled the withdrawal of the Mandate of Heaven from an imperial house, auguring the fall of a dynasty. Earthquakes were another sign. In July, a massive earthquake struck close to Beijing in Tangshan, flattening that city and killing hundreds of thousands of people. As aftershocks shook the capital, people whispered that Mao had lost the Mandate of Heaven.

Jiang Qing was reportedly irritated by how the earthquake and relief work distracted people from the more important task of criticising Deng Xiaoping.

* * *

Mao Zedong died on 9 September 1976, felled by his third major heart attack in five months. A complex, contradictory and often cantankerous figure, larger than life and all too human in his flaws, Mao was capable of the grandest revolutionary visions but also the pettiest manipulations. He was both an inspirational leader and a remorseless tyrant. The public mourned Mao's passing with visibly less fervour than they had Zhou's.

Jiang Qing and her cohort saw themselves as rightful heirs to power, their hubris blinding them to their unpopularity and the fact that the source of their power was gone. No one stood politely anymore when Jiang entered a room and they talked over her at meetings.

Hua Guofeng heard that she and her allies were plotting a coup. On 6 October, backed by others including Ye Jianying, now minister of defence, he summoned Jiang's three closest allies – Yao Wenyuan, Zhang Chunqiao and Wang Hongwen – to a meeting at Zhongnanhai, purportedly to discuss the publication of the fifth volume of Mao's *Selected Works*. Zhang and Wang were arrested on entry. Security forces separately arrested Yao and Jiang Qing.

The Cultural Revolution was finally over.

The new Party leadership blamed all the pain and suffering of the previous decade on this 'Gang of Four' – introducing Mao's phrase to the public for the first time. People joined the campaign to denounce the four with an enthusiasm they had not showed for political movements for some years. Some, however, held up five fingers. Even if Mao had not always agreed with the Gang of Four, they could have done nothing without their chief enabler.

PART FIVE

The Long Shadow of the Cultural Revolution

What will happen to the next generation if it
all fails? There may be a foul wind and a rain of
blood. How will you cope? Heaven only knows.

Mao Zedong

Mao's death and the arrest of the Gang of Four did not bring an
overnight change in rhetoric or action. Premier Hua Guofeng's
stated determination to uphold Mao's policies earned him the
unflattering label of 'whateverist'. In fact, he did far more to put
China on the path to economic, political and cultural reform
than he is usually credited for. He loosened the Party's ideological grip on culture and education while introducing the economic policies that are the basis for the post-Mao Reform Era
and for which Deng Xiaoping usually gets the credit.

The Party under Hua committed to the programme of modernisation first proposed by Zhou. This required cultivating
expertise, a quality Mao had denigrated in favour of ideological fervour, and involved both opening the country further
to foreign investment and, in 1977, reinstating national
university entrance exams. Six million people competed for
270,000 university places. Many came from the pool of what
by then was 16 million 'sent-down' youth, who saw it as their
last chance for a good education.

In 1978, the Party began posthumously 'rehabilitating'
many of the Cultural Revolution's most prominent victims,
including the playwright and vice-mayor of Beijing, Wu Han,
the Cultural Revolution's first official target, and the writer
Lao She, whose works returned to print and stage. It restored
the reputations of the late former defence minister and Great

93

Leap critic Peng Dehuai and President Liu Shaoqi, whose widow Wang Guangmei was released after twelve years of incarceration in 1979 – and who never forgave Zhou Enlai for not intervening on Liu's behalf. The Party brought others, including Xi Jinping's father Xi Zhongxun, back from exile or prison, giving them new positions in the Party and government.

Because the state still determined people's jobs and living arrangements, many victims were forced to live and work in proximity to those who had persecuted them. The Foreign Languages Bureau made Yang Xianyi editor-in-chief of the magazine *Chinese Literature* and honoured him and Gladys in other ways, but the couple could not escape contact with their former tormentors. Every part of the compound harboured traumatic memories.

Most Cultural Revolution radicals paid little or no price for their actions. Some even attained positions of power in the post-Mao era. Perpetrators of some of the worst atrocities went unpunished. Although Hua Guofeng conceded that the 'New Inner Mongolian People's Party' had never existed, no one ever had to take responsibility for the tens of thousands of deaths there, the 790,000 people falsely imprisoned, or the more than 100,000 people left permanently injured in the hunt for its members. In the case of Dao county, where organised mobs murdered thousands of men, women and children in 1967, only twelve people were prosecuted. All were given relatively light sentences – three years in some cases. Thousands of bereaved family members and other victims of injustice flocked to Beijing from across the country to petition for redress.

On 21 November 1978, the Party reversed the counter-revolutionary verdict on the 1975 Tiananmen Incident. Big-character posters expressing pent-up relief, grief, anger and demands for justice and change went up in places that became known as 'democracy walls'.

Beijing's Democracy Wall at Xidan, just west of Zhongnanhai, was the largest and most important, not least for its presence under the nose of the leadership. There, young people recited poetry, made speeches and argued for posthumous justice for victims including the young executed writer Yu

94

Luoke. They also distributed *samizdat* publications including the art-and-literature journal *Today*, whose circle (which included the artist Ai Weiwei) sparked an underground, or at least unofficially sanctioned, artistic and literary renaissance.

The Democracy Wall movement helped Deng and other reformist leaders demonstrate to recalcitrant leftists in the Party that the people would not tolerate any return to radicalism. At a historic Party plenum in December 1978, Deng outmanoeuvred Hua Guofeng, who remained the Party's nominal head, to become its dominant leader. The plenum formally adopted the 'Four Modernisations' as policy and set China firmly on the path of economic reform and opening its doors to the outside world. In early 1979, the Party finally closed the last of the May Seventh Cadre Schools. Washington and Beijing normalised diplomatic relations and Deng became the first Chinese Communist leader to visit the US.

A short-lived outlet for free expression: Democracy Wall at Xidan in Beijing, 1979

At Democracy Wall, a former Red Guard called Wei Jingsheng warned that without a 'fifth modernisation' – democracy – even Deng could become a tyrant like Mao. Just as Mao had packed the Red Guards off to the countryside once they'd outlived their usefulness, Deng shut down Democracy Wall and had Wei Jingsheng arrested as a warning about the limits of free speech.

The Party could afford to be more lenient towards the dissident dead. In March 1979, a Beijing court declared Yu Luoke

95

to have been 'innocent' and a provincial tribunal cleared the name of Zhang Zhixin, now officially a 'good Communist' and 'martyr' who had 'refused to give up in the face of death'.

Dealing with History

In 1981, the Party produced an official 'resolution' on the 'sixty years of glorious struggle' since its founding in 1921. The Cultural Revolution, which had been 'initiated and led by Comrade Mao Zedong', had 'led to domestic turmoil and brought catastrophe to the Party, the state and the whole people'. Mao had been bamboozled by the 'counter-revolutionary cliques' of Jiang Qing and Lin Biao, convenient scapegoats for a Party and a people reluctant to reckon with Mao's culpability or their own.

The Party took Jiang Qing and the rest of the Gang of Four to court, along with surviving associates of Lin Biao and a few other leading Cultural Revolutionary figures. It would henceforth be the role of the law, not the 'masses', to dispense justice, even if the masses retained their role as informants à la the Maple Bridge Experience.

During televised proceedings of the 1981 trials, an unrepentant Jiang Qing called the judge a 'fascist' and famously told the court: 'I was Chairman Mao's dog. I bit who he wanted me to bite.' She received a suspended death sentence. As guards dragged her from the courtroom, she shouted, 'Revolution is glorious! Revolution is not a crime!' Ten years later, suffering from cancer, she hanged herself in a hospital bathroom, reportedly defiant to the end. The others were given hefty sentences, though most would be released well ahead of time for medical or other reasons.

The court sent Red Guard leader Kuai Dafu to Qincheng Prison, where he formed a close friendship with Democracy Wall's Wei Jingsheng. Released in the late eighties, Kuai went to work in a factory. Later he went into business, made a fortune and lost it. Zhang Tiesheng, the 'hero of the blank exam paper', also went to jail. Some years after his release he founded an agritech company that gave him a reported net worth of over US$60 million by the mid 2010s.

Nie Yuanzi, the firebrand whose big-character poster had

Trial of the Gang of Four

inspired Mao's 'Bombard the Headquarters', also obtained early release from her seventeen-year sentence. In ill health, on crutches at the time, she only avoided homelessness thanks to a former student who found her a tiny flat in the capital. 'That poster brought me tremendous fame and prominence,' she later reflected, 'yet it also brought endless pain and torment for the rest of my life'.[59] She died in 2019 at the age of 98. Her death went unmentioned in the Chinese press.

With the state propaganda organs devoting so much energy to demonising and scapegoating Jiang Qing, one of the most common and historically predictable lessons drawn was that of the danger of giving women power. Among the few other women who had ever wielded significant power in China's long history was the controversial Qing Empress Dowager Cixi. The narrator of the popular 1983 film about her, *Reign Behind a Curtain*, pointedly blamed the entire 'national catastrophe' of the late nineteenth century on Cixi. The message was clear: the Cultural Revolution was all Jiang Qing's fault.

Playing Cixi in that film was a young actress on her way to becoming the queen of 1980s Chinese cinema: Liu Xiaoqing, who as a ten-year-old had stood in Tiananmen Square, awestruck at the sight of Mao. Liu also starred in another landmark film of the decade, *Hibiscus Town*. It portrayed a love story between two victims of the Cultural Revolution, which the film's director, Xie Jin, called 'that catastrophic age of blood, fire and persecution'.

* * *

To prevent any one leader again prevailing over the collective, the Party foreswore personality cults, abolished the office of Party chairman and introduced a two-term limit for the position of Party secretary-general and the reinstated presidency. It banned big-character posters and launched campaigns to encourage civility. Having dealt with the Cultural Revolution to its own satisfaction, it told the country to move on: 'Look to the future,' it commanded: *xiàng qián kàn*. As many a wit noted, the character used for the future, *qián* 前, was a perfect homonym for money, *qián* 钱. People could now follow what the Party was careful never to call the 'capitalist road', pull themselves out of poverty and better their lives.

Always a woman's fault

97

Society was demilitarising. As state-run factories gradually shifted focus from heavy industry to consumer goods, advertisements for face cream and medicinal wine appeared on billboards that not so long before bore quotations from Chairman Mao. Copies of the once ubiquitous Little Red Book disappeared from bookshops on orders of the Propaganda Department.

The much-loved writer Ba Jin, a former Party supporter and Cultural Revolution victim, was one of many who feared that it was dangerous to bury the past. Another Cultural Revolution, he warned, 'would mean the destruction of our nation'. He proposed building a Cultural Revolution Museum that would confront people with the evidence of those 'terrifying events' and 'repay the debt of the past.'[60] Other Cultural Revolution victims endorsed Ba Jin's proposal. The Party ignored it.

Undeterred, many people attempted over the years to establish various kinds of memorials, sometimes with the support of local officials. Despite efforts to preserve cemeteries such as one in Chongqing where five hundred victims are buried, mostly teenagers, many local memorials and burial grounds have been bulldozed, built over or placed under heavy security.

The 1980s: Spiritual Searching, Cultural Fever and a Turn to Humanism

The collapse of Maoism as a holistic belief system left a spiritual vacuum. As the Party's argument for legitimacy subtly shifted from the ideological to the managerial, people began to search for meaning in both Eastern and Western religions as well as spiritual practices like *qigong* and philosophies such as those of Nietzsche and the existentialists. They struggled to deal with the loss of ten years of their lives to what now seemed a shameful, collective mania, as well as feelings of victimhood, betrayal and guilt.

This struggle for meaning combined with the exuberance of release from the ideological straitjacket of Maoism sparked the 'cultural fever' (*wénhuàrè*) of the 1980s – an explosion of creative energy, artistic and intellectual exploration and literary experimentation. A briefly tolerated genre of 'scar literature' delved straight into the trauma, while ironic artistic movements played with the aesthetics of both propaganda and big-character posters. A generation raised on earnest hymns to Mao and the Party embraced the anarchy, sexual energy and release of rock 'n' roll. The freshly graduated 'Fifth Generation' of filmmakers, including Chen Kaige, Zhang Yimou and Tian Zhuangzhuang, would take Chinese cinema to international acclaim on the festival circuit, with many of their films reflecting directly or allegorically on their Cultural Revolution experiences.

Publishing houses, freed by the economic reforms to produce reading matter that sold, published everything from serious investigative journalism to the cheeky best-selling 'hooligan literature' of the writer Wang Shuo, a mix of satire and love stories that captured the general atmosphere of anomie. Guo Lusheng's poetry found new fans. Living in and out of mental institutions, he would go on to win the People's Literature Prize in 2001; he once remarked that being considered insane allowed him to be 'absolutely independent in thought and spirit'.[61]

Deng Xiaoping's wheelchair-bound son Pufang became the PRC's first disability activist, establishing the China Welfare Fund for the Disabled in 1984. Some 730,000 people had been permanently disabled as a direct result of Cultural Revolution violence. He pushed for change in a country that previously offered few educational or career pathways to disabled people and made no efforts at accessibility. In the 1990s, Deng Pufang expanded his activism to encompass intellectual disability and mental illness and in 2003 would be awarded the United Nations Human Rights Prize.

If one thing united many of these diverse thinkers, creators and activists in the immediate post-Mao era it was the spirit of humanism. A former Red Guard, Dai Houying, brought this previously taboo concept to the fore with her influential novel *Ah, Humanity*. She described how 'to my young and ardent heart, socialism and communism were a world of wonder and excitement. I honestly believed that our cause was just, that our future was bright....' In the end, however, 'I came to see that I had been playing the role of a tragic dupe in what was a mammoth farce.'[62]

The spirit of humanism

Deng Xiaoping led the Party's regular, futile attempts throughout the 1980s to clamp down on humanism and other such expressions of 'bourgeois liberalism' and 'spiritual pollution' with political campaigns, complete with billboard slogans and workplace and school 'study sessions'. These campaigns were generally unpopular, except insofar as they targeted rising anti-social behaviour and crime. Official abuse of privilege again became a talking point, as people with connections conspicuously enriched themselves while others had to work punishingly hard to escape the poverty caused by years of social upheaval and economic mismanagement.

In 1986 and 1987, students demonstrated in several cities against corruption and for causes ranging from greater academic and media freedom to later lights-out times in university dorms. After the Party's relatively liberal secretary-general Hu Yaobang refused to punish Party members believed to have supported the protests, he was forced to step down as Party chief, a post he'd held since 1982. When Hu died in April 1989, students streamed into Tiananmen with wreaths and banners and poems much as an earlier generation had flocked to the square to mourn Zhou Enlai. This evolved into a months-long, widely popular nationwide anti-corruption, pro-democracy and pro-media freedom protest movement, as well as a student-led occupation of Tiananmen Square.

Observers noted the influence of the Cultural Revolution on the style of protest. Student leaders made haranguing, heroic speeches in which they demonised their enemies. And yet, as Dai Qing has written, unlike the Red Guards, these young people were not the instruments of someone else's will. They were speaking for themselves. The Party, alarmed by this new version of 'bombarding of the headquarters', ordered in the army to clear the square.

In late May, as army units began massing in the outskirts of the capital, five retired generals openly petitioned against the imposition of martial law. One was Chen Zaidao, the former head of Wuhan's Million Heroes, who argued, 'The People's Liberation Army belongs to the people. It should not confront the people, much less suppress them.' He knew better than most where army involvement could lead.

On 3-4 June, the army moved in with tanks and automatic weapons. Soldiers slaughtered around 1,000 unarmed citizens who were trying to block their path to the square and wounded many others. Protesters in Sichuan, Shanghai and elsewhere also met with state violence. Those too young to remember the Cultural Revolution expressed shock that the People's Liberation Army could turn its weapons on the people themselves.

Yang Xianyi gave an interview to the BBC in which he described Deng and other leaders who'd authorised the massacre as 'fascists'. He refused to retract his words and the Party that had welcomed him as a member five years earlier now expelled him. Lois Wheeler Snow, who had once shared her late husband Edgar Snow's admiration of Mao, said that what happened in 1989 'just woke me up'.

The events of 3-4 June had a profound effect on the people of Hong Kong and Taiwan as well. The opening and cultural excitement of the 1980s had bred hope for their own futures as well as that of the mainland. The shock of the 1989 crackdown fed into anti-communist, pro-democracy and nativist sentiments in both places.

The Berlin Wall fell in November that year. The Eastern Bloc crumbled soon after and then the Soviet Union collapsed. The Chinese leadership, already shaken by the 1989 protests, were convinced that Gorbachev's policy of *Glasnost*, or 'transparency', which had allowed Soviet citizens to learn, speak and write freely about the horrors of the Stalinist period, had led to the fall of communism there. They determined that the same would not happen in China, where the wounds of the Cultural Revolution were still deep and fresh. Collapse of the Soviet Union

In the early 1990s, the Party launched an intense, ongoing 'patriotic education' campaign focused on the young. It centred on the 'century of humiliation' that began with the Opium Wars and ended with the revolution of 1949. The violent campaigns of the 1950s, the famine and the Cultural Revolution were glossed over. The 'bewildering complexity and almost unfathomable brutality' of the period made it increasingly hard to grasp even for survivors, many of whom never discussed their experiences with their children. Some chose to forget, as if 'the suffering somehow cheapened this world of newfound prosperity, a reminder that it was built on violence'.[63] Unreinforced memories grew dim.

The Party, which had already banned the publication of reference material on the Cultural Revolution in 1988, began locking away first-hand materials in inaccessible archives. When an ethnic Chinese librarian from the United States bought some Red Guard publications at a flea market in 1994, the police detained him for four months for planning to smuggle out 'state secrets'.

The economic reforms shredded the security net provided by the Mao-era planned economy. Unemployment rose as state enterprises 'rationalised' their workforces. As inequality grew between rich and poor, as well as between coastal areas and the interior, some looked back at Mao-era collectivism through a rosy lens.

Economic reform and Mao-era nostalgia

There was a brief fad in the 1990s for restaurants in cities such as Beijing that evoked the 'sent-down' experience – serving upscale interpretations of rough peasant food along with lashings of nostalgia in the form of Cultural Revolution posters on the wall and perhaps a rustic farm implement or two in the corner. Cultural Revolutionary culture, detached from its history, slowly reinserted itself into Chinese life as opera troupe staples, drinking songs and even disco tunes. Contemporary artists courted global interest with their subversive and paradoxical appropriation of Cultural Revolution imagery.

The 1990s saw the rise of a new Mao cult. The old revolutionary was repurposed for a new age, as a god of wealth in some places, in others a talismanic protector of taxi drivers. The popular understanding of Cultural Revolution history gradually became so unmoored from reality that for a time in the 2020s, Mao, Zhou Enlai and even Lin Biao impersonators found themselves in demand on the weddings-parties-anything circuit. One of the most popular social media and e-commerce platforms in the Chinese-speaking world at the time of writing bears the name Xiaohongshu – 'Little Red Book' (also known as Redbook or RED in English).

A Neo-Maoist movement, with which the Party maintains

an uneasy relationship, has arisen as well. Some Neo-Maoists are simply unreconstructed old Maoists. Others are young people disillusioned by the corruption, inequality, exploitation, and cut-throat competition of the current era. Both new and old Neo-Maoists idealise the Maoist era, including the Cultural Revolution, as a time of greater ideological purity, equality, purpose and principle.

On 25 December 2023, the eve of Mao's birthday, thousands of mostly young people descended on his birthplace of Shaoshan, in Hunan province. They marched through the town chanting 'To rebel is justified!' and 'There's no crime in revolution!' and held up signs proclaiming 'Down with the Capitalists' and 'We want to return to the Mao Era!' One independent Chinese commentator noted at the time that such young people were 'by no means a small minority.' In 2024, the *Collected Works of Mao Zedong* hit the bestseller lists.

The More Things Change...

Xi Jinping became the leader of both Party and state in 2012. Too young to have participated in the anti-Japanese or civil wars like his father's generation of Party leaders, his stories of toiling alongside the peasants in the countryside as a 'sent-down' youth are an important part of his own myth-making. In 2018, Xi abolished the two-term limit to office, presenting the possibility that, like Mao, he'd be leader for life. This violated a key tenet of the immediate post-Mao order, orderly succession: should something unexpected happen to Xi, the scene was set for a power struggle. That same year, the Party crowned him a 'core leader' and enshrined 'Xi Jinping Thought on Socialism with Chinese Characteristics for a New Era' in the Party constitution. Just don't compare him to Mao: that is expressly forbidden.

Also forbidden is 'historical nihilism' – telling China's history in ways that deviate from the latest official version, which blames 'counter-revolutionaries' for the Cultural Revolution's excesses. The Party discourages any further discussion. A small but tenacious cohort of independent historians nonetheless have fought to preserve the true history of the era, along with other sensitive topics such as the Great Leap and the famine of 1959–1961. They include documentary film-makers and contributors to *samizdat* publications with titles such as *Scars of the Past*. Wang Youqin, a former classmate of the controversial former Red Guard Song Binbin, has devoted her life to recording the stories of the victims.

There are also family historians. Yu Luowen, the brother of the executed critic of the 'bloodlines' theory, Yu Luoke, has kept his brother's memory alive with online memoirs. He was moved to find a 'hurricane' of sympathy for his brother's plight on the fiftieth anniversary of his execution in 2020. In an apparent dig at Xi Jinping, a Party 'princeling' (political nepo-baby), Yu Luowen has observed that bloodlines still appear to be a key to power in China today.

Orwell observed, 'The further a society drifts from the truth, the more it will hate those that speak it.' These inde-pendent historians and others have braved intensive surveil-lance, harassment and the threat of imprisonment to record personal testimonies from elderly survivors and witnesses and collect photographic and other evidence before it too dis-appears. Some, like Wang Youqin, have been forced into exile.

* * *

To characterise the past by its errors, Xi has asserted, would result in 'great chaos'. But if the Party could live with its errors, some former rebels could not. Just nine months after Xi gave a major speech in 2013 against historical nihilism, a farmer appeared on *Please Forgive Me*, a television show normally populated by straying spouses and prodigal sons. He was haunted by how as a student in the Cultural Revolution he'd accused a teacher of betraying Mao. The teacher had been beaten, humiliated and sacked. Other former Red Guards apologised privately or online to the people they'd tormented.

When Song Binbin's high school celebrated its 90th anni-versary in 2007 at the Great Hall of the People, she was hon-oured as an 'outstanding alumna'. The organisers even dis-played the iconic photo of her pinning a Red Guard armband on Mao. No one mentioned Bian Zhongyun, the teacher who was beaten to death. In 2011, however, the school discreetly installed a bronze bust of Bian. The following year, Song Binbin published a self-exculpating account of Bian's murder, sparking an online storm. Two years later she visited the school, bowed before the bust and acknowledged her responsibility for failing to stop the murder, begging for forgiveness. Song died in 2024 aged 77, still unforgiven by many.

Song Binbin (middle) bows before a bust of Bian Zhongyun at her former high school.

Not everyone was sorry. Qi Benyu, the last surviving member of the Central Cultural Revolution Leading Group, passed away at the age of 84 in 2016. His sole regret was that he still hadn't seen the 'dawn of communism', although he reportedly said Xi Jinping made him hopeful that day could still come.

Meanwhile, a new generation of fanatics has arisen, as pumped on nationalism as the Red Guards were on revolution, ready both online and off to 'struggle' those they deem to be 'anti-China elements' and 'traitors'. Outspoken survivors of that era have likened them to Red Guards. They may well think this is a good thing.

In 2024, the 'Little Pinks', as they are sometimes called, focused their ire on Netflix's *3 Body Problem*. The series was based on a hugely popular science fiction novel by the writer Liu Cixin. They were incensed that it opened with a depiction of a brutal struggle session that only appears in the middle of the novel and by the violent depiction of that era in general. In fact, Liu, who was born in 1963, had originally begun the book with the struggle session. But his editors insisted he bury the scene in the middle to get past the censors. 'The Cultural Revolution appears because it's essential to the plot,' Liu told the *New York Times*. 'The protagonist needs to have total despair in humanity.'

An Accounting

Mao launched the Cultural Revolution to keep the Chinese revolution from falling into stasis, to punish his critics, blood a new generation of revolutionary successors, destroy China's ancient traditions and make room for the creation of a new, socialist culture. It was supposed to imbue the nation with such a strong ethos of egalitarianism and self-sacrifice that corruption, bureaucratism and 'bourgeois tendencies' would forever be banished from China. Instead, it has become a cautionary tale that cannot be told, a radioactive memory and a source of multi-generational trauma.

It began with an argument in the cultural sphere and became a purge of Mao's enemies in the political realm. It turned Chinese people against themselves, saw the army preside over mass murder, turned cities into battlefields and villages into killing grounds. At times it resembled civil war.

During the decade-long upheaval, at least 4.2 million people were detained and investigated and 1.7 million were killed, according to official statistics released in 1984. Of these, 13,500 were executed as counter-revolutionaries and 237,000 were killed in factional battles. The rest were presumably murdered as 'class enemies'. In all, some 71,200 families were 'destroyed in their entirety'. Millions of people were left with life-changing injuries. Even according to the official account, believed conservative by independent historians, more people were killed in the Cultural Revolution than the total number of British, American and French soldiers and civilians killed in World War II.

The Cultural Revolution left China with but a sliver of its material cultural heritage. In Beijing alone, Red Guards destroyed 4,922 of the city's 6,843 registered 'places of historical or cultural interest'. They burned over two million books and three million artworks and pieces of antique furniture. Because no signs indicate where buildings have been reconstructed or statuary replaced, most Chinese born since the 1980s have little awareness of how much material heritage the Cultural Revolution stole from them. Airbrushing this history, for a Party that under Xi claims to be the guardian of traditional culture, is vital to its claim to legitimacy. When Chiang Kai-shek took 600,000 treasures from the Forbidden City to Taiwan in 1949, the communists fulminated about the theft. These now constitute the greatest extant collection of Chinese material cultural heritage in the world.

Mao intended the Cultural Revolution to spark global revolution. It inspired some of the most brutal insurgencies and regimes in modern history, from the Khmer Rouge to Peru's Shining Path.

Two shadows lie over the present. One is that of censorship, the command to forget, lest the past escape from control. The other is that of the Cultural Revolution itself, demanding to be remembered, lest the past rule the present.

Mangoes: A Postscript

In 2011, a former lathe worker at Beijing's No. 1 Machine Tool Plant, Wang Xiaoping, travelled to Vietnam for a holiday with younger colleagues. There were mangoes on sale everywhere. She couldn't get enough of the mango shakes. She told her younger colleagues how, during the Cultural Revolution, her bad class background had meant she couldn't go to university, which is how she ended up at the factory. One summer day in 1968, her factory celebrated the bestowal of one of Mao's precious mangoes on the vice-director of the factory's revolutionary committee. Wax copies of the mango were distributed to the workers at a meeting. She was incredibly grateful, she told them, to have been included, to have been considered 'a member of the revolutionary masses' if only for a few days. Her younger colleagues were incredulous. They responded, 'It's only a piece of fruit! People of your time! Really!'[64]

EXPLORE FURTHER

* * *

Nonfiction

A Cadre School Life: Six Chapters | Yang Jiang, trans.
Geremie R Barmé, 1982.
Born Red: A Chronicle of the Cultural Revolution | Gao Yuan, 1987
Forbidden Memory: Tibet During the Cultural Revolution |
Tsering Woeser, trans. Susan T Chen, 2020
*Hundred Day War: the Cultural Revolution at Tsinghua
University* | William Hinton, 1972
Life and Death in Shanghai | Nien Cheng, 1986
Mao's Last Revolution | Roderick MacFarquhar and Michael
Schoenhals, 2006
Shades of Mao: The Posthumous Cult of the Great Leader |
Geremie R Barmé, 1996
*The Killing Wind: A Chinese County's Descent into Madness
During the Cultural Revolution* | Tan Hecheng, trans. Stacy
Mosher and Guo Jian, 2016
*Victims of the Cultural Revolution: Testimonies of China's
Tragedy* | Wang Youqin, trans. Stacy Mosher, 2023
Zhou Enlai: A Life | Chen Jian, 2024

*

Fiction and Film

Balzac and the Little Chinese Seamstress | Dai Sijie,
trans. I. Rilke, 2000 (novella)
Farewell my Concubine | dir. Chen Kaige, 1993 (feature film)

*

Documentaries

Chung Kuo | dir. Michelangelo Antonioni, 1972
Morning Sun | dir. Geremie R Barmé, Richard Gordon,
Carma Hinton, 2003

IMAGE CREDITS

Integrated images:

p.1 (verso): Students put up big character posters in the street, Beijing, 1966/7. Courtesy of Harvard-Yenching Library/Wikimedia Commons. Image in public domain. p.10: Soldier 'Lei Feng' reads the works of Mao. File available via Wikimedia Commons under Creative Commons CC0 1.0 Universal Public Domain. p.12: *Long live the triumph of Chairman Mao's revolutionary line of literature and art!* Characters from the revolutionary operas. Poster by Ding Jiasheng for the Shanghai Theatre Academy, showing the Communist stronghold of Yan'an in the background. Public domain. p.18: A 19th-century illustration of the character Sun Wukong, the Monkey King, from *Journey to the West*. File available via Wikimedia Commons. In public domain. p.22: Swimmers honour Chairman Mao in Wuhan's annual Cross-Yangtze Competition, September 1967. Image released by China's official news agency (public domain). p.25: Tiananmen Square on 15 September 1966. Image in public domain, available via Wikimedia Commons. p.26: Red Guards wave copies of Mao Zedong's 'Little Red Book', Beijing, 1966. Author unknown. Image in public domain in China, available via Wikimedia Commons. p.31: Buddhist texts destroyed by Red Guards at Jokhang Temple, Lhasa, Tibet. Picture courtesy of The Tibet Museum Photographic Archive, Gangchen Kyishong, Dharamsala, India. p.37: Zhou Enlai photographed by Marc Ribaud. Courtesy of Giumet National Museum of Asian Arts, Paris, France. p.43: Rebel Red Guard factions march in Shanghai, 1967. The banner reads: 'Warmly hail the congratulatory telegram from the Central Committee of the Chinese Communist Party, State Council, Central Military Commission, Central Cultural Revolution Group to the revolutionary rebel groups in Shanghai.' Image via Wikimedia Commons under Creative Commons Zero licence (CC0) licence. In public domain. p.46: Wang Guangmei is humiliated at a denunciation rally at Tsinghua University, Beijing, 1967. Available via Wikimedia Commons under CC0 licence. p.50: Guizhou rebel faction on the march, 1967. The banner reads, 'The People's Liberation Army firmly supports the proletarian revolutionaries'. Image via Wikimedia Commons under CC0 licence. In public domain. p.54: Students at Beijing Normal University prepare big character posters denouncing Liu Shaoqi. Image in public domain, available via Wikimedia Commons. p.58: Students mass outside the British mission gates. Unknown author. Image via 6Park.com. p.65: Propaganda poster from 1968: 'A team of capital workers and peasants receive a precious gift from the Great Leader'. Available from Jordan Schitzer Museum of Art under CC0 licence, via Wikimedia Commons. p.70: Female member of military guard for US press delegation at airport in Beijing, 1972. Photograph courtesy of the Nixon Foundation. p.74: Wreckage of Lin Biao's crashed plane in Ulan Bator, Outer Mongolia. Author/credit: BJ Warnick / Alamy. p.77: Ping Pong diplomacy. p.78: US President Nixon and Mao shake hands. Official tour photograph courtesy of the Nixon Foundation. p.92: Caricature of the 'Gang of Four' from Lu Xun Art Academy, 1976. Poster courtesy of International Institute for Social History collection, via British Library. p.95: Democracy Wall at Xidan, Beijing. Author: Liu Heung Shing. Image courtesy of The China Project, New York. p.105: Song Binbin bowing © Han Wen.

Plate section:

p.1 (top): Teenagers perform revolution for the masses, Tiananmen Square, Beijing, 1966. Credit: Universal History Archive/UIG via Getty Images.

(right) Swimmers read from a book of Mao quotations before swimming in the Yangtze, September 1967. Author/credit: Li Zensheng, courtesy of The China Project, New York.

(left) Workers receive the gift of a preserved golden mango from Chairman Mao. Official postcard. Image in public domain.

p.2: (above) *Bombard the Headquarters – My Big Character Poster.* Official propaganda poster, Beijing 1966.

(below) 'The new culture', Red Guards perform a Official propaganda poster c.1966/7, in public domain.

p.3: (above) Chairman Mao meets Song Binbin in Tiananmen Square, 1966. Official photograph in public domain (colourised).

(below) Collectable figurine/propaganda art: a 'reactionary academic authority' submits to a struggle session, c. 1966/7.

p.4 (top): Chinese citizens carry a portrait of Mao. Official propaganda poster in public domain, collective work of the People's Fine Arts Publishing House Creative Group. Image via *The Mao Era in Objects* website courtesy of the IISH/ Stefan R. Landsberger Collection.

(right) Chairman Mao badge, c. 1969, metal and enamel. Inscription on reverse reads: 'Mao Zedong Thought is the lighthouse of the revolution.' Image (edited for clarity) via British Museum.

(left) *Chairman Mao goes to Anyuan.* Author/credit (original painting): Liu Chunhua, 1967. Official propaganda poster, in public domain. Image courtesy of IISH/Stefan R. Landsberger Collection.

p.5. Official postcard, c. 1968, featuring one of several Mao Zedong Steam Locomotives. Captioned 'The first train to cross the Nanking Yangtze River Bridge' on reverse. In public domain.

p.6 (above) Jiang Qing depicted as actress 'Lán Píng' (stage name), 1935. In public domain, via Wikimedia Commons.

(below) *The Red Detachment of Women* (1972 production). Official White House photograph by Byron Schumaker. In public domain.

p.7 (above) The Nixons visit the Great Wall of China, 1972. Credit: Getty Images.

(below) Workers perform in factory yard. Image in public domain via Wikimedia Commons.

p.8 Mao-era propaganda posters on display beside a street bookseller, Beijing, late 2010s. Image credit: Alamy.

(left) Red Guards at a rally in Tiananmen Square, holding copies of Mao's 'Red Book', February 1966. Image via Wikimedia Commons. In public domain.

(right) Tiananmen Square, 1989. 'Tank man' image credit: Jeff Widener/ Associated Press. Low-resolution image provided for fair use via Wikipedia under Creative Commons Attribution-ShareAlike 4.0 license.

SELECT ENDNOTES

1 See Chen Jian, *Zhou Enlai: A Life*, Harvard University Press, 2024, p. 549.

2 Quoted in Delia Davin, 'Gendered Mao: Mao, Maoism, and Women' in Timothy Cheek (ed.), *A Critical Introduction to Mao*, Cambridge University Press, Cambridge, 2010. p. 197.

3 See Daniel Leese, 'A Single Spark: Origins and Spread of the Little Red Book in China' in Alexander C Cook (ed.), *Mao's Little Red Book: A Global History*, Cambridge University Press, Cambridge, 2014, pp. 31–33.

4 Quoted in Roderick MacFarquhar and Michael Schoenhals, *Mao's Last Revolution*, Harvard University Press, Cambridge, 2006, p. 110.

5 Translated by Geremie R Barmé in 'History Writ Large: Big-character Posters, Red Logorrhoea and the Art of Words', *Journal of Multidisciplinary International Studies*, vol. 9, 2012.

6 See James Carter, 'Power of symbolism: the swim that changed Chinese history', *The China Project*, 14 July 2021; and David Bandurski, 'The Jury is Out: Mao Zedong Swam Faster than Today's Olympic Champions', *Medium*, 18 May 2016.

7 Quoted in Andrew G Walder, *Fractured Rebellion: the Beijing Red Guard Movement*, Harvard University Press, Cambridge, 2009, p. 149.

8 Quoted in Dick Wilson, ed., *Mao Tse-Tung in the Scales of History: A Preliminary Assessment Organized by the China Quarterly*, Cambridge University Press, Cambridge, 1977, p. 252.

9 Quoted in Tania Branigan, *Red Memory: The Afterlives of China's Cultural Revolution*, Faber & Faber, London, 2023, p. 92.

10 See Wang Youqin, *Victims of the Cultural Revolution* (trans. and ed. Stacy Mosher), Oneworld Academic, London, 2023, pp. 19–23.

11 See Roxane Witke, *Comrade Chiang Ch'ing*, Little, Brown, Boston, 1977, p. 323.

12 Translated in Andrew G Walder, Ibid., p. 150.

13 Liu Xiaoqing quoted in Geremie R Barmé, *Shades of Mao: The Posthumous Cult of the Great Leader*, M.E. Sharpe, New York, 1996, p. 174.

14 Wang Shuhua's story is told in the online footnotes to p. 16 of Geremie Barmé, *The Forbidden City*, Harvard University Press, Cambridge, 2008.

15 See Denise Y. Ho, *Curating Revolution: Politics on Display in Mao's China*, Cambridge Studies in the History of the People's Republic of China series, Cambridge University Press, Cambridge, 2017, p. 233–236.

16 Qian Liqun, quoted in Laikwan Pang, *The Art of Cloning: Creative Production During China's Cultural Revolution*, Verso Books, London, 2017, p. 9.

17 Li Yong, 'Wenhua da geming' zhong de mingren zhi yu (*The Imprisonment of Famous People in the 'Cultural Revolution'*), Central Nationalities Institute Publishing House, Beijing, 1993, p. 387.

18 Yan Fei, '"Turning One's Back on the Party and the People": Suicides during the Chinese Cultural Revolution', *China Journal*, vol. 91, no. 1, 2024, pp. 67–88.

19 See Geremie R Barmé, 'In a retro mood: The ethical dilemmas of cutting a deal with Xi Jinping's China', *The China Project*, 15 September, 2023.

20 See Yongyi Song, 'Chronology of Mass Killings during the Chinese Cultural Revolution (1966-1976)', *SciencesPo*, 25 August, 2011.

21 Quoted in Christian Sorace, 'Metrics of Exceptionality', *Critical Inquiry*, vol. 46, no. 3, 2020, p. 564.

22 Sang Ye and Geremie R Barmé, '"That which cannot be taken away" – Analects', *China Heritage*, 20 February, 2024.

23 See Dick Wilson, *Zhou Enlai: A Biography*, Viking Press, New York, 1984, and Chen Jian, *Zhou Enlai, A Life*, passim.

24 See Quan Yanchi, *Tao Zhu zai 'Wenhua Dageming Zhong' ('Tao Zhu During the "Cultural Revolution"')*, Central Party School Publishing House, Beijing, 1991, pp. 155-157.

25 Qi Benyu, *Qi Benyu huiyilu ('Memoirs of Qi Benyu')*, 2016.

26 Yu Luoke, 'On Family Background: the creation of a caste system in Maoist China', *Contemporary Chinese Thought*, vol. 32, no. 4, 2001, p. 35.

27 Nicolai Volland, '"Liberating the Small Devils": Red Guard Newspapers and Radical Publics, 1966-1968', *The China Quarterly*, vol. 246, 2021, pp. 354-373.

28 Ian Johnson, *Sparks: China's Underground Historians and Their Battle for the Future*, Oxford University Press, Oxford, 2023, p. 186.

29 David Milton and Nancy Milton, *The Wind Will Not Subside: Years in Revolutionary China, 1964-1969*, Pantheon Books, New York, 1976, pp. 196-197.

30 See Jonathan Spence, *Mao Zedong: A Life*, Penguin, New York, 2006, pp. 162-163.

31 See Delia Davin, Ibid., p. 213.

32 *Ni bu da ta jiu bu dao ('If you don't beat them, they'll never be overthrown')*, Lyrics and music, *Hongweibing shilu ('Facts about Red Guards')*, ed. Li Jinwei, Hong Kong World Overseas Chinese Society, 1967, p. 96.

33 See Daniel Leese, 'A Single Spark: Origins and Spread of the Little Red Book in China', in Alexander C Cook (ed.), ibid., p. 36.

34 See David Bandurski, 'In an Era of Laws, Who has a Rightful Claim to Mao's Millions?', *China Media Project*, 13 December, 2007.

35 See 'Wenge zhen xiang zhi Qinghai 8.18 qunzhong bei tusha shijian' ('The True Face of the Cultural Revolution in Qinghai and the Slaughter of the 18 August Red Guard Masses'), *Wenge yu dangdaishiyanjiu wang* (website).

36 Prime sources for this section are Yang Su, *Collective Killings in Rural China During the Cultural Revolution*, Cambridge University Press, Cambridge, 2011, pp. 37, 65, 69 and 151-52 and Yan Fei, '"Turning One's Back on the Party and the People": Suicides during the Chinese Cultural Revolution', *China Journal*, vol. 91, no. 1, 2024, pp. 67-88.

37 For an excellent record of contradictory exhortations by officials and official media see Julia Kwong, *Cultural Revolution in China's Schools, May 1966-April 1969*, Hoover Institution Press, Stanford, 1988.

38 Sources include Thomas Jay Mathews, 'The Cultural Revolution in Szechwan' in *The Cultural Revolution in the Provinces*, ed. Ezra Vogel, Harvard University Asia Centre, Cambridge, 1971, p. 101 and Tania Branigan, *Red Memory: The Afterlives of China's Cultural Revolution*, Faber & Faber, London, 2023, p. 118.

113

39 See Thomas W. Robinson, 'The Wuhan Incident: Local Strife and Provincial Rebellion during the Cultural Revolution,' *The China Quarterly*, no. 47, 1971, pp. 413-38.

40 On Kuai Dafu, see William Hinton, *Hundred Day War: the Cultural Revolution at Tsinghua University*, Monthly Review Press, New York, 1972, pp. 120-122 and 126-127.

41 See James Ross Corcoran, The Jingju-Wayang encounter: China and Indonesia during the Cultural Revolution and the Gestapu Coup and Countercoup (PhD diss., University of Hawai'i, 2005), p.376.

42 David Milton and Nancy Dall Milton, ibid., p. 271.

43 Edward E Rice, *Mao's Way*, University of California Press, Berkeley, 1972, p. 376.

44 Sources for eyewitness accounts of the events include official British archival sources and William Hinton, ibid., p. 132-4. For a complete list, see the PDF on the author's website.

45 The key reference used for this section on Inner Mongolia was David Sneath, 'The Impact of the Cultural Revolution in China on the Mongolians of Inner Mongolia', *Modern Asian Studies*, vol. 28, no. 2, 1994.

46 The researcher was Zheng Yi. See Yang Su, ibid., p. 152.

47 The list of weapons left behind comes from Jaap van Ginneken, *The Rise and Fall of Lin Biao* (trans. Danielle Adkinson), Avon Books, New York, 1977, p. 163. The account of the Hundred Day War comes from multiple sources including William Hinton, ibid., 1972.

48 Jian Guo, Yongyi Song and Yuan Zhou, *Historical Dictionary of the Chinese Cultural Revolution*, The Scarecrow Press, Lanham, 2006, quoted in Yongyi Song, 'Chronology of Mass Killings during the Chinese Cultural Revolution (1966-1976)', *SciencesPo*, 25 August, 2011.

49 Chen Jian, ibid., p. 597.

50 See Geremie R Barmé, 'The Trouble with Dai Qing', *Index on Censorship* 21.8, 1992.

51 Quoted in UPI, '1971 Year in Review: Foreign Policy: Red China and Russia'.

52 See Paul Clark, *The Chinese Cultural Revolution: A History*, Cambridge University Press, Cambridge, 2008, p. 105. Another catchy title belonged to the recorded tune 'Ensure that Literature and Art Operate as Powerful Weapons for Exterminating the Enemy', discussed by Andrew F Jones in 'Quotation Songs: Portable media and the Maoist pop song', in Alexander C Cook (ed.), ibid., p. 43, which is also the source of the Jiang Qing quote.

53 See Elizabeth O'Brien Ingleson, *Made in China: When US-China Interests Converged to Transform Global Trade*, Harvard University Press, Oxford, 2024, an excellent account of China's trade relations and the politics behind them in the 1970s.

54 See Maghiel van Crevel, 'Underground Poetry in the 1960s and 1970s', *Modern Chinese Literature*, vol. 9, no. 2, 1996, pp. 169-219.

55 Jaap van Ginneken, ibid., pp. 307-308.

56 The essential source for this section is Sebastian Heilmann, 'Turning Away from the Cultural Revolution: Political Grass-Roots Activism in the

Mid-Seventies', *Center for Pacific Asia Studies at Stockholm University*, Occasional Paper 28, September 1996, p. 16.

57 Roderick MacFarquhar and Michael Schoenhals, *Mao's Last Revolution*, Harvard University Press, Cambridge, 2006, p. 388.

58 Translated in Richard Curt Kraus, *Brushes with Power: Modern Politics and the Chinese Art of Calligraphy*, University of California Press, Berkeley, 1991, pp 132–135.

59 Chris Buckley, 'Nie Yuanzi, Whose Poster Fanned the Cultural Revolution, Dies at 98', *The New York Times*, 3 September 2019.

60 Ba Jin, quoted in Geremie R Barmé and John Minford (trans. and ed.), *Seeds of Fire: Chinese Voices of Conscience*, Hill and Wang, New York, 2nd edition, 1988, pp. 381–384.

61 Quoted in Wu, J, 'How the caged bird sings: Educational background and poetic identity of China's obscure poets' (PhD diss., Leiden University, 2021), p. 64.

62 Dai Houying, quoted in Geremie R Barmé and John Minford, ibid., pp. 157–160.

63 Ian Johnson, ibid., p. 224.

64 Wang Xiaoping, '1968: my story of the mango' in *Mao's Golden Mangoes and the Cultural Revolution* (Alfreda Murck, Yang Li and Ying Zhuang, ed.), Scheidegger & Spiess, 2013, p. 44.

ACKNOWLEDGEMENTS

This book was written on the unceded land of the Gadigal people of the Eora nation.

I am deeply grateful to all those who have taken precious time from their own work to read the book in manuscript and provide so much useful feedback and excellent suggestions. They include Geremie R Barmé as well as Xue Yiwei, Matthew Galway, Dan Tebbutt and Stacy Mosher (editor and translator of some of the key works I have cited here). I also want to thank those who have helped with research and such tasks as taming the endnotes: Sumina, Eva Huang, Seren Heyman-Griffiths, Lily Cameron and the incomparable Jade Muratore. The collections of materials on the Cultural Revolution at the Australian National Library, including original Red Guard publications and songsheets, have been invaluable, as was the privilege of being made a Petherick Reader there, and I have also drawn on the considerable resources of the State Library of New South Wales. Rebecca Fabrizi of the UK's Foreign Office shared a wealth of materials on the burning of the British Mission in Beijing in 1968 and helped to solve the mystery of which Peter Sellers film British diplomats were watching when the Red Guards stormed the place.

Any errors are my own.

Major sources used include Wang Youqin's *Victims of the Cultural Revolution*, Roderick MacFarquhar and Michael Schoenhals' *Mao's Last Revolution*, both Dick Wilson and Chen Jian's biographies of Zhou Enlai, Roxane Witke's *Comrade Chi'ang Ch'ing*, David Sneath's work on the Cultural Revolution in Inner Mongolia, Thomas W Robinson's on the Wuhan Counter-Revolutionary Incident as well as the work of Denise Y Ho, Andrew G Walder, Jonathan Spence, Julia Kwong, Christian Sorace, Laikwan Pang, Sheila Melvin, Jindong Cai, Ian Johnson, Tania Branigan, David Bandurski as well as, of course, Geremie Barmé. I have also referred, judiciously, to first-person accounts in English and Chinese.

I am deeply grateful to publisher and Great Helmsman Ben Yarde-Buller for proposing this fascinating project, and to him and all his colleagues at Old Street, especially revolutionary model editor Digby Lidstone, for being both wonderfully rigorous and great fun to work with. A big thank-you, too, to Kieron Connolly of Old Street. The early enthusiasm of Zha Ji-anying, Paul French and Kerry Brown for this book has meant the world. I am delighted that my old comrades at Black Inc are co-publishing the book in Australia, and it has been a joy to work once more with Sophy Williams as well as Amelia Willis and Laura Blundy Jones there. Thank you to my revolutionary cover designer James Nunn in the UK and Beau Lowenstern in Australia. If I could do a loyalty dance to my agent Gaby Naher, I would. Josemi is my comrade on the Long March.

For a complete list of references and endnotes, please go to *https://lindajaivin.com.au/books/bombard-the-headquarters/* or scan the QR code below:

GREAT  EVENTS

Great Events are short, lively books of narrative history, written by experts but aimed squarely at the general reader, about the most dramatic and consequential events of the past 150 years. In time, we hope *Great Events* will offer an indispensable 'map of the territory', helping readers to follow their interests and chart their own course through the past.

For more information please write to the publisher at
info@oldstreetpublishing.co.uk